CHENG AND THE GOLDEN PHEASANT

THE BIOGRAPHY OF
CHENG TSO-HSIN
BY YANG QUN-RONG

Professor Cheng Tso-hsin.

iii

Working on bird collections in the Institute of Zoology, Chinese Academy of Sciences.

iv

CHENG AND THE GOLDEN PHEASANT

THE BIOGRAPHY OF
CHENG TSO-HSIN
BY YANG QUN-RONG

TRANSLATED BY ZHANG ZHENG-WANG,

DING CHANG-QING AND

SIII JIAN-BIN

World Pheasant Association-International

Fujian Science and Technology Press, Fuzhou,

Fujian, China

First published in China by Fujian Science and Technology Press, Fuzhou, Fujian, China in 1993

Published in the United Kingdom by the World Pheasant Association, PO Box 5, Lower Basildon, Reading, Berks RG8 9PF, 1995 and Fujian Science and Technology Press, Fuzhou, Fujian, China

British Library Cataloguing in Publication Data

A catalogue record for this book is available from the British Library

ISBN 0 906864 20 8

Cover illustration: Golden pheasant photograph by Jean Howman
Cover design: Tom Gardiner

Printed in Great Britain by Hartnolls, Bodmin, Cornwall

ACKNOWLEDGEMENTS

The Biography of Cheng Tso-hsin is translated from the Chinese edition published in March 1994 by Fujian Scientific Publication Press. We would like to thank the editor, Mr Hu Shan-mei, and the author, Mrs Yang Qun-rong, for their permission to translate it from Chinese to English. Our thanks also go to Mr Keith Howman, who suggested this translation; Prof Cheng Tso-hsin for kindly providing photographs and other material; Mr Zhao Zhong-ying and Ms Bao Ting with the translation; and the English teachers of Beijing Normal University, Ms Liping Lo and Mr George L Ganat, for reading most parts of the book and helping us to correct some of the grammar. Derek Bingham has done a splendid job as Editor and our thanks go also to Jean Howman for her Golden Pheasant photograph on the cover.

CONTENTS

Publishers introduction   xi

1.   Early years   1

2.   University days   21

3.   Golden pheasant   42

4.   Marriage and early field research   53

5.   Back to America   69

6.   The Chinese bird list and the
      Revolution   76

7.   Bird research   87

8.   Public criticism   112

9.   Germany and the Soviet Union   116

10.   Chinese birds and zoogeography   124

11.   Overseas visits   150

12.   Editing and teaching   194

13.   Miscellany   213

14.   Perfect companions for a golden
      marriage   233

15.   Time waits for nobody   245

The chronicle of Prof Cheng Tso-hsin   252

Selected ornithological publications   258

PUBLISHERS INTRODUCTION

Professor Cheng's biography written by his daughter-in-law, Yang Qun-rong, was sent to me in early 1994 at a time when I was giving thought to special events to mark the 20th anniversary of the founding of the World Pheasant Association. What could be more appropriate than to publish an English version of the biography of our remarkable President.

Correspondence began with Joe Cheng, as he became known in America and he and the original publishers all agreed to our publishing an English version.

The next problem was the translation of the original into English and this was undertaken by Zhang Zhengwang, the Secretary of the World Pheasant Association Chapter in China together with colleagues Ding Chang-qing and Shi Jian-bin. It was a major task for them.

Finally the editing for a Western audience and this was carried out by Derek Bingham who has made his skills so freely available to the Association over many years. We owe him, Zhang Zhengwang and colleagues a great debt of gratitude.

As this biography makes clear, Professor Cheng is a most extra ordinary man to throw up an excellent job because a quite extraordinary perception - to achieve academic distinction at the age of 23 in 1930 in America was an extraordinary achievement for a Chinese person at that time. To challenge the thinking of Chairman Mao on the damage done by sparrows was a brave act of academic integrity. To complete this introduction I asked Professor Cheng to tell us a little more than his biographer had of the golden pheasant and its influence on his life.

K C R Howman

June 1995

CHENG AND THE GOLDEN PHEASANT

The male golden pheasant is one of the most magnificent and beautiful species of gamebirds throughout the world. It is adorned with a golden-yellow crest of disintegrated silky feathers and a conspicuous cape of golden-orange fan-feathers. The back is metallic green, turning to golden-yellow towards the tail; the lower body is mostly scarlet; and the tail rather long, somewhat arched, the central tail feathers black profusely spotted with buff. What a gorgeous pheasant it is!

The golden pheasant was the one of the first bird species identified and described by Linnaeus in 1758. The county near the place of its origin has been named 'Treasure Pheasant County' after it. In natural distribution, it is indigenous to China, and Europeans have been importing the living bird from China ever since 1740.

It is a very popular species as an aviary bird. The China Ornithological Society has chosen the bird to be its emblem. It has also symbolic of the economic development now in progress in China.

The golden pheasant was the bird which attracted me to ornithological work. It has been the bird species which has so much influence on my ornithological career and is no doubt the reason I have encouraged so many splendid young Chinese field ornithologists to work on galliformes in general and pheasants in particular during the past two decades. For a scientist, the important thing in life is not only to be persistent in research and education but also to pave a path of further development for future generations. My favourite motto is 'KIP', 'keeping it positive' with the magnificent achievements and aspirational strategy of the World Pheasant Association.

Ever onwards!

Cheng Tso-hsin, ScD
(Michigan 1930)

Research Professor of Ornithology
President Emeritus, China Zoological Society
President Emeritus, China Ornithological Society
Academician, Chinese Academy of Sciences
President, World Pheasant Association
11 March 1995

THE EARLY YEARS

After the Opium War in 1840 the imperialists, with their strong armies and powerful weapons, opened the door to China. Fuzhou, the capital of Fujian Province, soon became one of the five big trading ports in China. A succession of foreign businessmen came to Fuzhou to make use of the cheap labour and the abundant resources to open their factories. A great number of tea mills, sugar refineries, printing houses, paper mills and shipyards were established. The Chartered Bank and the Hong Kong Shanghai Banking Corporation established branches in Fuzhou. Missionaries also came and built their churches. They claimed that they would help Chinese people become free from hardship and lead their souls into Heaven. In fact what they brought was abnormal prosperity with endless bullying, humiliation, mortification and hardship. However the Chinese people were not willing to see their country divided and oppressed. They struggled heroically against the invaders and explored ways to remove the sources of poverty and backwardness in China.

In April 1911, the Huang Hua Gang Uprising led by Dr Sun Yat-sen and Huang Xing, both great Chinese revolutionaries, suffered defeat. The bad news spread to Fuzhou, which made the spiritless air above the city even more depressed and people more agitated. However, it also predicted a new storm would soon come.

In a suburban district near the Gu Mountains lived a Cheng family. One day the scene in the courtyard was of pandemonium. Many people had gathered, their faces showing sorrow and concern. Inside lay Chen Shui-lian who, although only 27 years old, was having a very difficult time breathing because of serious pulmonary tuberculosis. Although on the verge of death, she struggled to hold onto her life until her husband came. A few minutes later, Cheng Sen-fan arrived, having had to endure the hardships of a long journey back from a far part of the country. Chen Shui-lian opened her eyes and gazed at her husband with deep love, muttering to him with her last strength, "Please bring up our son and daughter......." Then she left the world.

There was great confusion in the room, cries mingling with shouts. Cheng Sen-fan's five-year-old son, Cheng, could not understand what had happened and why dad, grandma, uncle and aunt cried so loudly. He caught hold of his grandma's clothes and asked "mama is still sleeping, why doesn't she wake up?" No one had either the time or the will to tell him about the death, frightened of hurting his innocence. Little Cheng continued to cry "I want mama! I want mama!" He could not understand that he had lost his mother who was so gentle, quiet, refined, dignified, beautiful and well-educated. Cheng's younger sister, Cheng Hui-zhen, was only three years old at that time. She was too young to understand.

Cheng Sen-fan, Cheng's father, was more than 30 years old. He was one of the few intellectuals who had received higher education, having graduated from Fuzhou Yinghua Academy (similar to a modern college). Because he wanted his children to receive a good education in Fuzhou, he moved his family from Changle county to a suitable place near the Gu Mountains.

The students of Yinghua Academy and particularly Cheng San-fan, were very good at learning English. As a result it was not difficult for him to find a job in the Salt Bureau. A scribe in charge of writing reports and making documents, he was also sent by his supervisor to many parts of the country to handle business matters. He had been to quite a few counties in Fujian province as well as to Jiangsi province, Hunan province, Zhang Jia Kou city in Hebei province and Bao Tou city in Inner Mongolia.

Cheng Sen-fan was an honest man who worked conscientiously. He was always on the move and found it hard to find time to be at home with his family for even a couple of weeks. Now after the funeral of his wife, he had to leave home again. He had no alternative but to entrust his mother with the duty of looking after his children. Thus it was that, now over 50 years of age, she became responsible for bringing up her grandchildren.

Cheng's grandma was in excellent health at that time. As well as managing household affairs, she also did needlework which she sold exclusively for additional income. Her kind face was always smiling and she never reprimanded her grandchildren. On one occasion she and Cheng, hand-in-hand crossed a small bridge in the village. Some children from rich families were eating lychees, a fruit from southern China, and Cheng shouted and asked for some lychees as well.

Grandma told him that he must learn to become a scholar rather than compete with the other children in eating and dressing. Then she bought some lychees for him although she herself begrudged eating even one of them.

The kindly-faced grandma was intelligent and eager to learn. Although she had not gone to school, she knew many words and could read some simple books. It seemed that she had a wealth of knowledge for she had memorised many stories, such as *Changer flew to the moon* (The lady Changer who swallowed an elixir stolen from her husband and flew to the moon), *Eight immortals crossing the sea, The match of a turtle and a hare, Zheng Huo cruising to the Western Oceans, The foolish old man moving the mountains,* and so on. Every night, she always told her grandson several marvellous stories before he fel asleep. Among them, Cheng's favourite was *Jingwei fills up the sea with pebbles*. He often asked his grandma to tell him this story again and again.

"Long long ago, there was a God of the Sun. The God had a daughter, named Nuwa. Nuwa was very beautiful, with pretty eyebrows and bright eyes, and clever and brave as well. The God of the Sun loved his daughter and wished that she would stay with him. But Nuwa wanted to travel everywhere on the earth, to see the outside world and to play in far-away places.

"One day, Nuwa got a small boat and went to sea. The wind had dropped and the waves were calm and Nuwa's small boat drifted easily on the sea. She felt very comfortable, for it seemed as though she was sitting in a cradle or lying in her mother's arms. But when the sea lost its temper, the waves roared like an angry wild animal, tossing the small boat up and down. But brave Nuwa was not frightened.

"On another day, Nuwa once again paddled the small boat out to sea. The sea suddenly turned hostile: the strong wind was howling, the black waves lapping against the sides of the boat. The small boat was like a leaf in the ocean, and Nuwa battled the winds and waves with all of her energy. Finally, a huge wave came, the small boat turned over and Nuwa drowned.

"After her death, Nuwa changed into a bird. The name of this bird was Jingwei. Jingwei was beautiful, with a white bill and a pair of bright red feet. She built her nest in a high mountain on the north side of the sea. She vowed her revenge by filling up the sea. The

6

sea heard about it and sneered: "I am so big and you, Jingwei, are so small. It is only a dream that you want to fill me up. It is a boast that you say that you can fill me up." Therefore, the sea shouted at Jingwei, who nested in the woodland "Do as you please! Why should I fear you?"

"Jingwei said nothing but began to look for materials to fill up the sea. She picked up a pebble and next a twig. From morning till night, she continued her work, filling up a bit of the sea on one day and a little more the next. Day by day, year after year, over a long period of time, she filled the sea up more and more. And the sneer of the sea became lower and lower, weaker and weaker. Finally the voice of the sea had nearly disappeared. Jingwei married a Petrel, another alluring seabird. They had two children, one daughter and one son. The boy looked like his father, while the girl looked like her mother. They also joined in filling up the sea with pebbles. They were afraid of neither the strong wind nor the huge waves. They flew back and forth, holding the pebbles in their mouths, filling up the sea again and again, without stopping...".

His grandma always stopped at this point and asked Cheng, "What do you think of Jingwei? Is she good or not?" Cheng was fascinated by the story but he did not answer, instead, he questioned her closely, "grandma, is Jingwei still filling up the sea with pebbles?" Although many years have passed, Jingwei is still flying in Cheng's imagination. The unyielding spirit of the bird impressed him greatly. This story, and many others which his Grandma told him, inspired in him a love of nature and aroused his desire to gain knowledge. He looked forward to swimming in the ocean of science and technology.

* * * * * *

With the best care and the good teaching of his grandma, Cheng grew up healthily. He was not fat, had a pair of bright piercing eyes and a good looking and cheerful face. He liked small animals, enjoyed making chalks with lime water, and although he could not read, he liked to imitate adults by holding a book in both hands.

There were many different types of book in his father's book case. They became Cheng's elementary primers. When he found pictures of animals or plants in the biological books he would ask his grandma "What is that flower? What is that bird? Do you think the bird can fly?" Once, Cheng found a picture with some men and women drawn on it and asked, "What is man? What is woman? What are the differences between them?" Grandma could not answer all his questions at once.

Later, Cheng discovered books on other subjects such as Chemistry, Physics and even Mathematics. Although he could not read them, he was interested in looking at the pictures and drawings and he never stopped asking his Grandma questions about them. Grandma paid attention to encouraging her grandson's good habits. She trained Cheng to return books to the place he had taken them from, to keep the room clean and tidy. She didn't allow her grandchildren to leave things lying around wherever they liked.

Cheng still remembers his grandma's teaching and keeps the good habits learned in early years. In his office all documents, books and materials are kept in order so that he can easily find any one he wants to use. Even today, at the age of 88 and despite leaving the office many years ago, he can still remember the location of all his books and materials. If he wants to use one of them, he will ask his wife or his students to take it out for him, and they will easily find the book by following his instructions. At present Cheng works at home and keeps materials in order in his study. His family knows never to move his materials.

When he was nearly six years old, Cheng went to the Cang Xia Zhou Primary School. Everyday he was happy to go to school by himself and during class he listened to the teachers carefully. His teachers praised him as a good student because he observed the class rules very well. After class, he went back and reviewed what he had learned at home. When he knew about 1000 Chinese characters, he began to read supplementary books to extend his knowledge. Grandma knew Cheng was eager to read, so she discussed with her son the possibility of sending Cheng to a private school to learn classical Chinese literature after he finished his class at the Primary School. Cheng's father agreed. When his father came home, Cheng proudly recited some poems with his hands clasped behind his back:

"The sun beyond the mountains glows;
The yellow river seawards flows.

You can enjoy a grander sight, by climbing to a
greater height."
"This morn of spring in bed I'm lying,
Not woke up till I hear birds crying.
After one night of wind and showers,
How many are the fallen flowers!"
"Before my bed a pool of light,
Is it hoarfrost upon the ground?
Eyes raised, I see the moon so bright;
Head bend, in homesickness I'm drowned."

Looking at his clever, eager-to-learn, smiling son,
Cheng Sen-fan gained great consolation knowing that
he was being raised properly.

There is no way of knowing precisely how many
classical Chinese literary charactors Cheng learned
and memorised in his childhood. But there is no doubt
that he benefited greatly from the very good
elementary knowledge of classical Chinese he
obtained in his early years when he subsequently
began his research work. For instance he had no
difficulty in reading *Shijing* (*The book of songs*, a
Chinese work written 3000 years ago), *Qinjing* (*The
book of birds*) and other classics.

After graduating from primary school, Cheng went to study in a middle school attached to Fuzhou Youth Organisation. At night, apart from completing the homework which the teachers assigned to him, he read other books as well. Usually he worked with a candle until midnight. His grandma was now getting old and, because she worked very hard during the day, she went to bed earlier. If she woke up after midnight, she always found Cheng still reading and usually urged him to go to sleep.

On one occasion when grandma woke up at midnight, she saw Cheng holding a book in one hand and a stick in the other, reading while pointing at the wall. She thought that he must have done something wrong, so she got closer and discovered that Cheng was studying Geography by using a map on the wall. His method of learning Geography thus made him not only get a good mark in this course, but also laid a foundation for him in elementary knowledge of the subject. It is probably the reason why he made such a great contribution to the field of zoogeography.

As a result of studying day and night, Cheng became very thin. He looked pale and weak and one day whilst reading a book, he felt dizzy and fainted.

Grandma was frightened and asked a neighbour to telegraph Cheng's father who returned quickly. After inquiring about Cheng's studies, he decided to talk to his son.

He sat in front of Cheng's bed and asked

"How are you feeling now?"

"Much better."

"How many days have you not gone to school?"

"One week."

"You are so young, but you have been ill for a week. In the future you will go to university and study much harder, and you will be far busier than you are at present. If you do not have a healthy body, how can you do that? In the future, when you have graduated from college, you will work for the country for 30 to 50 years. How can you do that without a healthy body?"

Cheng thought that what his father said was quite reasonable. Father saw his son listening to him conscientiously. He then told him stories about some famous people all over the world who always did some type of physical exercise for good health. Finally, he stressed, "if you want to study well, you must exercise; if you wish to take on great responsibilities, you also need to make sure to exercise. Do you understand?"

"Yes, I agree!" Cheng replied seriously.

From that day, Cheng exercised vigorously. Everyday he walked to school. It took him an hour to get there and back. People always saw him on the playground. He liked to play football and volleyball, but his favourite was table tennis. He held the table tennis bat in his left hand (he is left handed) and with both a hard half-volley and overpowering smash, he usually won the game. While growing up he also liked to play tennis and continued this after he became a professor. Even today, he still keeps a pair of tennis rackets in his house.

Because he exercised frequently, Cheng was soon in excellent health and became robust. In his last year of high school, Cheng competed in the games. Since he was not quite 16 years old, he was placed in the Youngsters Group. The school permitted each student to enter no more than three track and field events. So Cheng entered for the 100-metre dash, the long jump and the triple jump. The results were:

"The champion of the 100-metre dash is Cheng Tso-hsin."

"The champion of the long jump is Cheng Tso-hsin."

"The champion of the triple jump is Cheng Tso-hsin."

Cheng won three gold medals, became the best athelete in the school and was awarded a silver cup to the congratulations of his classmates and teachers. Winning three trophies had aroused in Cheng the enthusiasm to continue physical training. After that he spent his spare time playing football, volleyball, tennis, track and field events, climbing mountains and walking, and he also enjoyed many sports. When his father came back again, he was very pleased to see Cheng's silver cup and to celebrate his son's achievements he invited all the family to a picnic in the countryside.

Cheng's father, Cheng Sen-fan, was an intellectual who had received a very good education. He was very receptive to new ideas, and his ideas more or less influenced his son. The good physical condition obtained during middle school was essential for Cheng's research work in later life. At 50 years of age he was still able to climb Huang Shan Mountains to undertake bird research. At 70 he reached the

Heavenly Lake of Changbai Mountains, which is 2600 meters above sea level. All of these accomplishments were due to his physical training in his early years.

* * * * * *

Cheng Tso-hsin loved nature from childhood. He would collect small animals, plants, flowers and grasses, even lichens and mosses and collections in the bookcase and drawers changed very often. He particularly liked to catch the amphibious crab, a small crab living in the wetland areas, both for food and for fun. The riversides and pool banks, where the crabs lived, became the places which he haunted.

Cheng kept up his hobby of catching amphibious crabs into middle school. Even when he entered college, he spent spare time fishing for crabs after class. Children in the north normally used their hands while Cheng, born in the south, caught them with a fishing rod. He became very proficient in his early years. When he had a good 'harvest', his grandma would reward him by cooking a delicious crab sauce, the left over crabs being kept in water so that Cheng could observe their behaviour.

16

Nevertheless Cheng was even more interested in the colourful birds in the forests. He could identify many birds by calls from his studies in primary school. His house was located near the Gu Mountain which was not only very beautiful but where there were many birds. He often climbed the mountain with his young friends and played hide-and-seek in dense forests.

There was a large temple named Young quan Si in the Gu Mountain which is famous for its springs. Water coming from them is cold, very clean and has a distinctive character. Rich people would come to the temple in sedan chairs to burn incense and pray, normally taking nearly half a day to reach the temple from the foot of the mountain. Yet it took Cheng less than half a day to go up and down when he competed with his classmates. When he stopped to rest at half way, he would enjoy the beauty of the colourful flowers and the various grasses and watch insects and birds in the surrounding forest. He benefited from climbing mountains not only in extending his field experience but also in relaxing from hard study.

Cheng and his classmates had heard that there was a cave at the top of Gu Mountain in which tigers could frequently be heard roaring. Cheng wanted to visit Tiger Cave to see if there were tigers in it or not. One weekend he agreed with his classmates that they would stay in the Yong-quan Temple for the night and then try to reach the summit the next day in order to explore the secrets of the cave.

On the day, at first light, they began to climb Drum Mountain. Looking upward from the Yong-quan Temple, the summit of the mountain looked as if it was just behind the hills and it seemed that they could reach it in a few hours. At the start everyone talked and laughed, ran and jumped with great vigour and enthusiasm while climbing. Although the mountain was very steep, they were very confident. However, as soon as they were over one hill another, higher hill appeared in front of them. Up and down, down and up they went until they had climbed several hill tops. But there were still many ahead of them. The mountains became higher and higher, steeper and steeper. Some of them were frightened and decided to return to the temple and then back to town.

Cheng was also very tired, soaking wet and short of breath. But he recalled the story of the bird Jingwei filling up the sea, which re-invigorated him. He made

18

up his mind that he would not give up. The team became smaller and smaller until only Cheng and one classmate remained. They finally reached the summit before sunset.

There they saw a huge stone shaped like a drum. This is why the mountain is called Gu mountain; Gu means a drum in Chinese. Soon they found a cave, from which, suddenly, loud and horrible noises emerged Cheng and his classmate were very frightened. But no tigers came out. A few minutes later, the same noises were heard again and after they had heard it time and again they finally found the secret of the Tiger Cave.

Because Gu mountain is about 1000 meters above sea level, strong winds often cross the summit which when they go through the cave, create the loud noise which in the far distance sounds like a tiger roaring. Farmers in this area did not know what it really was and dared not come too close to the cave.

So the rumour that tigers lived in the Tiger Cave of Gu mountain was created and spread by many people. It was Cheng and his classmate who first discovered the secret. It became darker and darker. Cheng and his classmate should have gone down the hill earlier and it was too late for them to return the way they had come up. Looking down, Cheng saw a small path on the other side of the summit. They followed it arriving at the Yong-quang Temple within an hour.

Afterwards, although Cheng realised that if they had known of this small path earlier it would not have taken them a whole day and so much energy to climb the mountain, he felt very happy to have this expedition under his belt and was very impressed by the experience. At the same time, he learnt two important truths: whatever one does, one will succeed if one is persistent; whatever one does, one should not do it without clear understanding and planning for if one knows the situation in advance, one will get twice the results with half the effort.

UNIVERSITY DAYS

At that time students normally studied in the middle school for six years. Yet it took Cheng Tso-hsin only four years to finish by skipping two grades. Was it his father's help? No, his father had just been transferred to be principal of Jiangzhe Middle School in Hunan province. He seldom came home. Was it his teacher's partiality for him? As a matter of fact all the teachers who taught him liked this intelligent and diligent student and they often gave him additional homework so that he could learn more. But they did not give him preferential treatment. There was no intention of giving him high marks or lowering standards.

Cheng studied really hard, in his spare time teaching himself advanced lessons. If he did not understand, he would consult reference books. Thus, he not only passed all the examinations, but also skipped one grade for his outstanding performance. Skipping another grade was much easier. After another final exam the following year, one teacher was visibly pleased after marking his examination papers. So were the other teachers, who were united in their praise of him. When the examination papers reached a teacher in the upper grades, he meticulously went over them and was even more impressed: "It seems that he has grasped the essentials better than my own students. Why not allow him to skip another grade?" Cheng skipped again. Therefore it was not surprising that, at the age of 15, he had finished all of the courses and graduated from high school. Then he applied to enter Fujian Christian University, one of the best colleges in China at that time. During registration a short, thin, childish-looking candidate appeared. The administrator at registration glanced at him and asked,

"Who are you registering for?"

"For myself."

"Which grade are you in?"

"I have graduated from the high school."

"Really? Then, how old are you?"

"I am fifteen."

"What is your name?"

"Cheng Tso-hsin."

The administrator believed that this was an unprecedented case, and asked the principal for instructions. The principal made the decision without hesitation: Cheng was too young to register.

22

On hearing the news, Mr Zhu Le-de, the headmaster of the high school where Cheng studied, wrote to Fujian Christian University. In it he praised Cheng Tso-hsin and recommended him to the university, asking them to give Cheng a chance. He suggested that the university should consider Cheng as an ordinary applicant: if he could pass the entrance examination, the university should accept him; if he failed the university could then refuse him. Since Mr Zhu was of noble character and had considerable prestige in both the city and the province, Fujian Christian University accepted his request. Thus Cheng got the chance to take the entrance examination. When he went to the examination room, the chief examiner and some of the others cast doubtful looks.

But they were completely wrong. They were greatly surprised when Cheng received a high grade. After his examination paper was handed in, an examiner looked it over quickly and exclaimed, "Surely, he will be enrolled." The event which made a stir was Cheng performance in the English examination. His written translation was quick and accurate. His oral translation was fluent. At last, the examiners could not help showing smiles of satisfaction and they congratulated him. How did Cheng learn English? He began when he was five years old. First, he learned words and expressions for everyday use, and then gradually he learned how to read, his initial teachers being his father and uncle.

His uncle had frequent contact with foreigners and could speak very good English. He liked his hard-working and clever nephew very much. He often took him to his house and taught him some English.

After he went to school, Cheng spent all of his spare time reading and remembering English. He always got the highest marks in English tests. Cheng had another advantage in learning English. His cousin, the son of his uncle Chen Jishan, was a senior engineer of the American Automobile Manufacturing Factory. He often sent presents of foreign records which Cheng would listen to with his uncle. If it was a song, he would try to learn the words. If it was a poem, he would try to write down the sentences. To him, listening to the records was not only a way to enjoy the art but also a way to practice his English. With this help plus his hard work, it was natural that his English was so good.

The College Entrance Examination papers were brought to the president of Fujian Christian University. After reviewing Cheng's test paper very carefully, he was convinced that Cheng was indeed qualified for entry. Breaking the rules, he decided to admit him. Thus, Cheng Tso-hsin, still like a small child, strutted into Fujian Christian University, full of hope.

* * * * * *

Fujian Christian University was located in Kuiqi village in Gu Mountain. Ringed by the Min River and the Gu Mountain, the campus comprises beautiful buildings arranged pleasantly inside the university. It was even better than a park: it was an ideal place to study. Cheng Tso-hsin cherished this rare chance to study, making the best use of his time, and the special credit system of Fujian Christian University as well. His original study abilities, formed in high school, were given free rein.

At that time most of the textbooks used in the university were written in English and the professors taught mostly in English. Since Cheng was good at

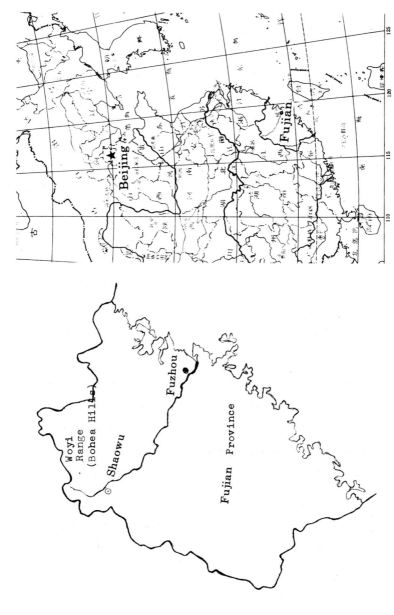

Map showing the location of Beijing and Fujian province, Fuzhou and Shaowu cities and Wuyi Range (Bohea Hills)

26

English, it was to his benefit, and he usually applied to take the tests early and gained extraordinary marks. Consequently it took him only three-and-a-half years to finish the usual four-year course and he received his Bachelor degree in the spring of 1926 at the age of 19. Once as a freshman in a biology class, Professor Kellogg asked, "What kind of fruit contains the most vitamins?" No-one could answer in the first row. When it was Cheng's turn, he replied, "tomato." Kellogg was very pleased and asked him his name. Professor Kellogg remembered Cheng's name and often encouraged him to study hard. His encouragement was a spur for him to major in biology in his sophomore year.

As a freshman Cheng wanted to study both biology and chemistry as he had not decided which one to choose as a major. Kellogg's encouragement compelled him to choose biology, which subsequently became his life's work. Although Cheng received the highest mark in the biology class, in fact he knew nothing about the tomato except its name. He just happened to have read a US textbook and remembered the name and he wanted to know more about it.

After graduating from the university, Cheng went to the United States of America to pursue his advanced education. When the boat stopped at a harbour in Japan he went off to buy some fruit. At a stall, he caught sight of a red round fruit, just like a Chinese persimmon. He brought some back and shared them with his friends. Although they looked like persimmons, they had a different taste, being sour and tart and everyone who ate them looked doubtful. They began to discuss what were they eating. Seeing this, a sailor from Guangdong province told them that they were American and were nutritious. But because he could not speak English, he did not know their name.

When Cheng arrived in San Francisco he went ashore for lunch. Once again he saw the red persimmons. This time there was an English label beside them on which was written tomato. At last, this was a tomato! Later, the tomato was imported into China and was called Fan Qie in southern China and Xi Hong Shi in northern China. In fact the tomato was originally found in Peru where the inhabitants regarded it as poisonous and called it the Wolf Peach. In the sixteenth century, an English traveller to Peru admired its luxuriant foliage and red fruits and brought it back to England.

Later he dedicated it to Queen Elizabeth I. From then on, although the pleasing-looking Wolf Peach was planted in botanical gardens around the world, no one dared to eat it. In the eighteenth century, a French painter was so lured by the Wolf Peach's inviting looks that, having painted it, he decided to risk eating it. To his surprise, several hours afterwards he was still alive and feeling very well.

At the time when Cheng answered Professor Kellogg's question correctly, he did not realise that the tomato would influence his career choice. But he was enlightened by the story of the tomato. He thought that, on the way to scientific research, there must be all kinds of frustration but if one's work is really valuable, sooner or later it will be recognised by the public, as the tomato was. So one should continue steadfastly on the path of discovering the truth.

* * * * * *

In his childhood Cheng Tso-hsin was not only fond of playing in the mountains, catching shrimps and fishing, but also catching and playing with snakes. He had a clever way of catching them which enabled him not to be hurt by them.

But once he did endanger himself. He was catching snakes at the foot of Gu mountain. He had seen one in front of him and was just about to catch it when he became aware of something moving behind him. Turning around quickly, he was confronted by a cobra, lurching towards him with its long tongue stretched out and its venomous fangs visible. He knew that this kind of snake was extremly poisonous and that 90 percent of people bitten by it die. Swiftly breaking off a branch he struck the snake with all his might. The cobra stopped and fled in panic. Cheng Tso-hsin drew a lesson from this: never be careless, even when doing familiar things.

As a child he had learned that most of the beautifully-coloured snakes were poisonous, while most of duller-coloured snakes such as brown or black ones, are less likely to be poisonous. He was even more confirmed in this view since it was written in his high school biology textbook.

One day after he had gone to Fujian Christian University he was climbing Gu mountain with his classmates when suddenly there was a cry of "snake!" All of the students save Cheng drew back instantly whereas he went up to observe the snake carefully. When he saw that it was brown and black and had no ringlike marks on it, he exclaimed confidently "Don't be afraid! It is not poisonous." Then he caught it and happily handed it to the zoological professor who was with them. But the professor was so terrified that he ordered the students to kill it at once because, he explained later, it was venomous.

The death of the snake made Cheng wonder. He remembered it clearly written in the book, the characteristics of the poisonous snakes: beautiful coloured skin, triangular head, some ringlike specks on the body. But that dead snake did not have such features. Why? he asked the professor. The professor told him that the characteristics written in the textbook are only normal cases. This snake is a special one: although its colour and marks were not so obvious, it was nevertheless poisonous. He also told Cheng that he might want to perform a chemical experiment to show whether it was poisonous or not. Cheng did so and it turned out that the snake was indeed poisonous.

This greatly impressed Cheng. He believed that one should read books because they were the summarization of previous experiences. However, one should not believe them totally and uncritically, because the world is a changing place and everything in it is changing; it is necessary for us to turn to nature, keeping in contact with realisties, and at the same time, to learn from experienced people and our teachers. Later in his research work he followed this motto.

For all the years Cheng travelled throughout China researching in the wild, in sunshine or rain, unafraid of wild animals or of poisonous snakes he was seeking something new, something which had never been written about in textbooks before.

* * * * * *

Having graduated from high school, Cheng Tso-hsin was keen to pursue his advanced studies in the United States. But his family was not wealthy, and could not afford the high travelling expenses. Fortunately his uncle Cheng Shou-xin sponsored him. Cheng Shou-xin was first a nurse in Fuzhou Hospital and had then taught himself to become a Chinese doctor and he earned good money. He was willing to pay the travelling costs because Cheng Tso-hsin was very clever and studied hard. So in 1926, when he was only 19 years old, Cheng travelled far across the sea. He reached the United States after two weeks and was admitted by the Biology Department of the Graduate School of the University of Michigan in Ann Arbor, one of the top ten universities in the United States. He majored in Zoology.

Cheng Tso-hsin never forgot his uncle's help during this hard time. After he returned to China and became a professor, he always supported his uncle and later his cousins lived in his home for over ten years. The affection between the uncle and the nephew was always very strong.

One reason why Cheng chose the University of Michigan was that it was a public school and charged relatively lower tutition fees. The other reason was that his cousin in the United States, Chen Jishan, was a senior engineer in the Buick car-manufacturing plant in Flint, Michigan. Chen Jishan had been sent to the US to study by the Chinese goverment after he graduated from Qinghua University. He majored in

33

car-manufacturing at the Massachusetts Institute of Technology and was later employed by Buick. Cheng went to the graduate school of Michigan to register for the entrance examination, with his recommendations and transcripts, and passed without a problem. Then he became a graduate student of Biology.

Passing into the University was quite easy for him, but how to remain there became a problem. Cheng was a complete stranger in the United States. Cousin Chen was very busy. He could only spare one or two weekends per month to see him and take him to a Chinese restaraunt to have a good dinner. Chen Jishan was not able to subsidize his living costs and Cheng's living and study expenses were totally dependent on his part-time work.

It was not difficult for him to find work because his English was very good. His first job was washing tubes for one or two hours every day in a hospital. This made him start studying after eight o'clock in the evening. There were many courses from which he could choose. The assistant director helped him choose a major. With his help, Cheng chose embryology since it was regarded as the most advanced subjects. He also took courses in genetics,

34

evolution and taxonomy. Later when he had more spare time, he took some other courses, such as paleaontology, zoogeography and the German language.

Everyday he tried to learn more and not to waste any time. Prof Okkelberg was Cheng's tutor and he was proud to have a Chinese graduate student. When he discovered that Cheng was not financed by the Chinese Government and wanted to find a proper part-time job to pay for tuition, he let Cheng do odd jobs in the biology department, such as catching frogs for the experiments, preparing for experiments, and cleaning the laboratory after they were over. But because this work took Cheng too long he had to find another job of nursing in the hospital near the university.

One year later, the biology department appointed Cheng to rear white mice. The big ones and small ones were kept in separate cages. Everyday, he had to mix feed, keep the cages clean, make sure the mice were healthy, record their movements, mating practices, and death. The quantities of the white mice in the cages were always changing, with changes happening in more than 100 cages. Every day he had

35

to go on a two-hour tour of inspection, once in the morning and again in the evening, feeding and recording. He was very busy, his studies were very hard, he did not have any free time at all. Cheng was very strict with himself: he must study well in order to do well in the tests and must not make any mistakes in rearing the white mice.

It was later that Cheng learned that these white mice were involved in cancer research. In the 1920s cancer was already a popular research subject. Scientists studied the cause of the disease and the method of controlling it through experiments on the white mice. Most American students were not willing to look after the mice for fear of cancer, but Cheng did it nonetheless.

Because Cheng had such excellent marks, he was later appointed to be research assistant by the graduate school. Having a regular salary, he did not need to do any other work. Another year later, he was awarded a scholarship by the graduate school. At the same time, the Chinese Science Culture Education Committee also awarded him a research stipend. Therefore he no longer had to do extra work for a living and could totally concentrate on his studies.

The University of Michigan at Ann Arbor is a beautiful campus. But it was also a rigorous school where students worked very hard and played hard too. Sports were popular although there is no physical education requirement. The most popular sport was football at Michigan. The students used to purchase a book of football tickets at the beginning of the term so that they could watch all the football games. It was expected that all the students should watch the intercollegiate football matches in which the Michigan team competed. There would be a ceremony when the school team entered the arena, with the brass band performing the school song. Sometimes even the president attended the grand ceremony.

At the beginning of the school term, Cheng was too busy to watch the matches and wasted a lot of tickets. Later when he had more free time, he went to watch some of the matches and came to like it very much. Football is a rough sport. It was very popular at that time in the United States and the Michigan school team was well known.

Cheng clearly understood that without a healthy body he would not be able to finish the rigorous courses. It was essential for him to do physical exercise. Therefore, he always played tennis with his classmates and his skill improved a great deal, so he had more energy to do the research.

During the four years at the University of Michigan, he always led a simple and frugal life. He rented a ten-square metre apartment, which was very small and was not equipped with any appliances, so he had to have his three meals on the street. In the morning, he normally ate some cookies for breakfast, then went to attend classes. At noon, he ate only two hot-dogs and drank a cup of milk and another cup of orangeade. In the evening, he would go to a Chinese restaurant to have some noodles or some rice. Only when his cousin came to see him could he eat something really good. But he did not care about it. His aspiration was to save China by science, so his arduous circumstances were not unbearable to him. In fact he never had any wish for sumptous living conditions. He just devoted himself to scientific research, and prepared to write a high quality thesis.

* * * * * *

Cheng Tso-hsin majored in Developmental Biology (Embryology) which was considered one of the most advanced subjects at that time. He also studied Animal Taxonomy, Paleogeology and other related courses. During the two years in the Graduate School he had some papers published in the College journal such as *Intersexuality in frogs, Some new cases of intersexuality in tadpoles, Hypogenitalism in frogs.* Subsequently, he obtained a Masters Degree.

In the following two years, Cheng made some new discoveries while studying the development of the germ-cells in frogs. Because of this research he wrote his graduation thesis on *The germ-cell history of the frog: I. Origin of germ-cells and formation of gonads; II. Sex differentiation and development.* This thesis was selected and sent to a German scientific journal, *Zeitschr. f. Zellf. u. Mikr. Anat.,* to be published.

In the second decade of the twentieth century it was accepted that science and technology in Germany exceeded that of the United States by far, so it was somewhat unusual for a German scientific journal to publish a thesis that came from the United States. Cheng's thesis was not only published in Germany but intrigued German scientists greatly. It was regarded as a masterpiece, a comprehensive and profound study of the embryo. It also advanced some original ideas. It was lucid and written with ease and grace and attracted much and widespread praise.

What impressed the German scientists greatly was that the author was a young Chinese scientist. At that time Chinese biological science was no more than a barren land. Therefore the Chinese name of Cheng Tso-hsin that appeared in the European and American science forum became well known and he was warmly congratulated by his supervisor and his classmates.

In June 1930 the president of the University of Michigan presented Cheng with his Doctorate Degree and at 23 years of age Cheng came to be the youngest doctor in the University. The biology department gave him a special prize, the Sigma Xi Key Award, a gold key in a brocade box.

Sigma Xi Key is a credit award presented by the United States graduate schools in order to encourage exceptional students. It means that they can use this golden key to open the gate of science and technology. Cheng was very excited. The Sigma Xi Key strengthened his resolve and confidence to scale new heights in science and technology.

He treasured the Sigma Xi Key very much and still cherishes it today. Through many difficult years he and his wife have had to sell valuable things in order to live but not the golden key. Even during the "Cultural Revolution", when their house was searched and their property confiscated, they still tried to keep the key. To Cheng, the Sigma Xi Key was not only a reward but a symbol of encouragement to scale new heights. It was also an encouragement to others.

THE GOLDEN PHEASANT
CHANGES HIS LIFE

The University of Michigan had a museum which housed a collection of wild animals in which biological specimens from all around the world were displayed. For Cheng Tso-hsin it became a place to relax during his stay there. Yet although the collection added greatly to his knowledge, there was rarely any one specimen that could inspire him mainly because, good as they were, most were only found in the United States. Then one day he caught sight of a splendid bird, a golden pheasant from China! The golden pheasant is dark gold on the back, red on the abdomen and orange-brown on the neck. The fan-like wings are like a shawl, the tail feathers very long and yellow alternating with speckled brown.

The sight of the golden pheasant provoked Cheng to deep thought. He thought of Baoji (golden pheasant in Chinese) county in Shenxi province in China and imagined this beautiful, long-tailed golden pheasant spreading its wings at the top of Qingling mountains and on the bank of the Wei river, then flying into the bright blue sky of its homeland.

Cheng had heard that there was a knoll Baoji county called Golden Pheasant Hill. He had also heard of a legend of the golden pheasant. Once there were four golden pheasants flying. They stopped in front of a steep and beautiful mountain which was later called Golden Pheasant Hill. Until then it was clear that three of them were males and the other was the sole female. A bitter fight took place between two males. They fought and fought. At last, the winner proudly displayed and soared high and the loser ran helter-skelter. While the winner was savouring his victory, the third male pounced. Another bitter fight ensued. In the end, a final winner appeared. It cheered its own victory again and again, to the admiration of the female golden pheasant.

It was well known that the golden pheasant is only found in China, so it is the Chinese who should study it. However it was first discovered by a Swedish biologist who gave it a Latin scientific name *Chrysolophus pictus* Linnaeus in accordance with international rules. Cheng was homesick and seeing the golden pheasant he could not help wondering why all the Chinese biological specimens were collected and named by foreigners.

Was it because the Chinese were not wise enough? Absolutely not! Our ancestors started to study birds much earlier than westerners. In the *Book of Songs*, the first Chinese collection of poems and songs written about 3000 years ago, there are about 100 references to birds and the first line of the first poem allurs mating calls of birds. There are even more references to birds in *Er Ya*, a book written during the Han Dynasty which is about 2000 years earlier, and in the Chinese scientific masterpiece *Compendium of Materia Medica*, written by Li Shi-zhen in 1596. It provides irrefutable evidence that China was one of the earliest countries to study birds. Why, then, did China lag behind?

Cheng concluded sadly that the underdevelopment of scientific education in China was caused mostly by corrupt government and a strained economy. He remembered when, in 1919, at the age of only 13 and in primary school, the reactionary northern warlords were preparing to sign the humiliating treaty in the Paris Peace Conference. It was violently rejected by people throughout the country. In Fuzhou, workers went on strike, merchants refused to trade, teachers

44

and students stopped having classes in order to display their anger. Cheng had watched the protest march in the street in which people destroyed Japanese commodities. He hurried home to tell his grandma and urged her to destroy all Japanese things in their house.

Later, led by the upper grade students, he also took part in meetings and listened to speeches. He began to understand what was happening and started to care about national affairs. In the May 4th Movement, Cheng took part in the student strike and the protest march. Under the influence of the foremost intellectuals, he came to believe that in order to save his backward homeland, people must rely on modern science. Consequently he chose the science-shall-save-China method. He resolved to win credit and honour for China.

Full of patriotism, he looked at the golden pheasant. He reasoned that the golden pheasant is an endemic species of Chinese bird and a Chinese person is the most eligible person to study it. He made up his mind to fill the blanks in Chinese science and to promote Chinese ornithology. This would mean changing his major study from embryology, about which he was familiar and had already achieved much, to a subject strange to him and which had received little attention in China. It also meant that he would lose the advanced equipment and conditions in the United States research institute and have to give up the excellent salary and material benefits he enjoyed in the United States. His tutor had already recommended him as a teacher in the University and the United States research institute and had hoped he would continue researching there. At the same time, the Fujian Christian University also invited him to return to his *alma mater* to work.

Pondering the matter over and over, Cheng decided to accept the invitation from the Fujian Christian University and go back to Fuzhou. He thought that because he was Chinese, he was the most eligible person to study the birds of China.

* * * * * *

In September 1930 Cheng Tso-hsin returned to the home town he had yearned for day and night. No great changes had taken place there, but the campus of Fujian Christian University, which he had left four

46

years previously, was orderly and tidy.

The president of Fujian Christian University welcomed Cheng warmheartedly, invited him to be a professor of the University and appointed him to the position of chairman of the department of biology. Since he was the first professor in the history of the university with a doctorate earned from an overseas university, his salary was even higher than that of the president who ran the university. Because of the limited number of teachers in the department of biology, Cheng taught general zoology at first and then specialized in teaching vertebrate biology, embryology and related subjects.

The teachers in Fujian Christian University normally gave lectures in English. This was not a problem for Cheng as he had studied in the United States for four years where his supervisor had praised him for his excellent English and thought that his thesis was even clearer than those of his American counterparts. That Cheng could speak fluent English was helpful to his students who were able to improve their own English writing and comprehension.

However teaching in English may cause difficulties for freshman new to science. So Cheng tried to give lectures in Chinese - a move warmly welcomed by his students. Although his lectures had substantial content as he often cited the latest progress in science as well as his own experiences, they were widely acknowledged as being well-organized, concise and inspiring. His classes were happy ones. The students liked to attend them not only because they thought the teacher had a sense of humour and his lectures were lively and interesting, but also because they believed that they could learn something.

His reputation spread quickly. An increasing number of students in the other departments also sought to attend his classes. Sometimes the room became so crowded that even a larger room could barely accommodate all of them. But however big they were, good order prevailed. Cheng thoroughly enjoyed giving his lectures because the students were so responsive - so much so that they usually overran their allotted times. His classes were so memorable that, in 1992, on his 86 birthday party held by schoolmates of Fujian Christian University, some of his former students who are now over 70 could still remember the impact he made over 50 years ago.

Recently he received a letter from Professer Qiao Yuan-chun, one of his former students now in the United States. In it Qiao wrote "When I was a freshman, I attended your lecture on biology and it was the most impressive class I had ever had. During that year, I also took part in birdwatching in the field early in the morning. Now 50 years have passed since then..."

Cheng not only taught in Chinese but also wrote textbooks in Chinese. Many teachers in Fujian Christian University had been invited to the United States, so textbooks, reference materials to scientific research, equipment and chemical reagents used in the experiments were also imported. In order to make the specimens in the experiments match the contents of the American textbooks, the university had to even import the same earthworms and frogs whose arteries and veins were imbued with different coloured medicament according to textbook descriptions.

Cheng thought that this was not necessary for his experiments he replaced imported specimens with local ones. He also suggested using the native language to teach in missionary schools. He made up his mind to practice what he preached and to compile practical textbooks in Chinese.

A year later Cheng had finished his first college textbook in Chinese *The Laboratory Manual of General Biology for use in Universities*, and it was published by the Commercial Publishing House in 1932. It was the first biological textbook written in Chinese for domestic colleges. He followed this with *General Biology, The Outline of Vertebrate Taxonomy* in Chinese. They were adopted as textbooks by departments of biology in many universities. In the 1970s, it was discovered at a book exhibition in Beijing that *General Biology* had been published in Taiwan seven times, which shows its far-reaching influence.

It was not easy for Cheng to compile the textbooks in Chinese at that time, because of the overwhelming popularity of things foreign. It was even more difficult for him to get them published. Yet he was supported by most of his students, who appreciated and understood his immense patriotic zeal.

* * * * * *

When he taught in Fujian Christian University, Cheng

Tso-hsin founded the university's Biological Society. At weekends or on holidays he often went, with colleagues and students, to the mountains or the wetlands to collect biological specimens. He thought everyone should learn from the book of nature.

On several occasions the Biological Society organized expeditions to Chuanshi, a small island about 15 kilometres in circumference outside of the mouth of Min river. Facing the Taiwan Strait and adjoining Wuhu (five tigers) Rockies, Chuanshi island seems like a guard at the door of Fuzhou. On it were several small hills, ruins of a telegram station, a meteorology station, old forts which had been used against the imperialists' invasions, many grottos in the hillside, bat-caves and the Celestial Cave of legends. Various plants grow on the island, sea eagles soar in the blue sky making harsh cries and there are flocks of birds. Surrounding the island, there are many fishing vessels.

Arriving by boat, Cheng and the other members of the society began to climb the hillocks or went into the sea to start their research. At ebb tide, they would be busier than ever for there were many molluscs, blood clams, several kinds of shellfish, snails and other invertebrates. Sometimes an argument would take place between an oystercatcher and a snipe, which made them recall the proverb that "when the snipe and the clam grapple, the fisherman profits. It is the third party that benefits from the tussle". There was also a large number of parasitic crabs on the beach.

The beautiful island attracted many scholars; Cheng and his fellow-members enjoyed their expeditions there, not only collecting many biological specimens for the university but also learning a lot from nature. They also often visited the wharf there. When the fishing boats arrived, they would try to buy some fresh fish and shrimps. Although they could not be identified by the biology teachers, they were much more interesting and lively than those drawn in books or displayed in the specimen collections. The natural world is a great book that nobody ever finishes reading.

Anthem of the Biological Society of Fujian Christian University.
Words by Cheng Tso-hsin; tune by Ren Qi-hui.
Published in Biological Bulletin vol.3:1 (1941)

MARRIAGE AND EARLY FIELD RESEARCH

When Cheng Tso-hsin started to teach in Fujian Christian University he lived in the university living quarters. Whenever he was on holiday he would go to the city to see his grandmother, who was living with Cheng's stepmother in the centre of Fuzhou. At that time Cheng's younger sister, Cheng Hui-zhen, was still studying in the South China Woman's College, while his younger brother, Cheng Tso-guang, and another younger sister, Cheng Mao-li, who were both born by his stepmother, were studying in middle school. His grandma was still well but she did want to see Cheng married.

Cheng was not only very handsome, but had the confidence and knowledge from having studied in the United States. Many people came to his house and introduced girls to him but he had his own ideas of the ideal companion.

He did not want to marry a girl from a rich family, or a girl who was gorgeously dressed and paid too much attention to her appearance. Instead, he wanted a girl who was solemn, gentle and quiet, who could share the same ideas with him. Although there were several pretty girls in the university who were well disposed toward him, none of them could attract Cheng's attention. Soon however, it became known that he had quietly fallen for Chen jia-jian, a young teacher at the primary school attached to the University.

Chen Jia-jian was pretty, very slim and 1.62 metres tall which was quite unusual among the girls in southern China. With a clean skin, a beautiful round face, a pair of big eyes, two big black plaits behind her head and dressed simply in a light blue cheongsam (a traditional Chinese woman's dress with high neck and slit skirt), she carried herself with dignity. She never looked right or left while walking.

Behind her back some boys in Fujian Christian University praised her as "a girl whose eyes are able to smile". She always firmly made a detour, with a smile, around those who blocked her way; and to those who would ask her the time in spite of having their own watches, Chen Jia-jian would simply tell them and move quickly on.

One day a lecture at the university had lasted

almost four hours and the speaker had long since lost the attention of many students who were passing in and out and even whispering to each other. Only Chen Jia-jian sat patiently listening all the way through, which was noticed by Cheng and impressed him deeply.

Later Cheng got to know Jia-jian very well and thought that she was the most beautiful girl in the world and much more lovely than those who wore too much make-up.

The window of Cheng's room faced onto the road which Chen Jia-jian walked down when she went to work. Soon she found that, every time she stepped on the dew-wetted stone road, there was always a young professor with books under his arms coming out of the dormitory and greeting her politely. When she returned home at dusk on the same road, there was the same professor, dressed for tennis and with a tennis racket in his hand, coming towards her. Chen Jia-jian found it difficult to pay no attention to the young professor with the air of a scholar.

One evening in 1932, Chen had bought some longans (a fruit which grows in the south of China) on the way home. On meeting Cheng, dressed as usual for tennis, she offered him some. Cheng accepted readily, holding the tennis racket horizontally so that she could put the longans onto it. Looking at the girl, Cheng was so excited and so nervous that he forgot to thank her. But Chen Jia-jian had felt a strong quake in her shy heart.

Chen Jia-jian was born in 1913 in Fuzhou, the daughter of a teacher at a missionary agricultural and technical school. He had four sons and five daughters and among his children, Jia-jian was the fifth. Life was hard in her childhood. She had a gentle disposition, was clever and eager to learn, intelligent and deft. Her father having died of overwork when he was still young, Jia-jian's family lived with her elder brother, who was working in the customs service, and her elder sister who taught in a middle school. After graduating from Wenshan Secondary School, Jia-jian registered at the Fuzhou Children's Normal School, where she had free tuition because of the poverty of her family. She was one of the best students in the school and, in 1930, graduated with excellent marks. She was then recommended by her headmaster to teach in the primary school attached to Fujian Christian University. At the time she was 17 years old.

In the school, Chen Jia-jian taught grade one. She was good at teaching music, painting and telling stories. Not only the students, but the principal and other teachers liked her very much. However, she always thought that her education was limited and she sought to continue her studies. Several years later, with some savings and a grant from churches, she continued her studies at the department of family affairs at Jinling Women's University.

At that time weddings were not the business of the bride and groom, but of their parents. Cheng asked his friends help him to go to Chen Jia-jian's family to act as matchmakers. Jia-jian's elder brother and sister took the decision as her mother had died earlier. They both agreed to the marriage.

In January 1935 the wedding took place in a small auditorium at Fuzhou Children's Normal School. Chen Jia-jian wore a pink cheongsam with white veil and was escorted by the best man and bridesmaid. Cheng, glowing with health and radiating vigor, wore a black Western-style suit. Many teachers and students of Fujian Christian University attended the wedding although there were also those who commented that a highly paid professor marrying a low-paid primary school teacher was not a good match.

But Cheng knew that what he wanted was a companion for life and Chen Jia-jian was ideal because she was industrious, virtuous and good-natured. Now, 60 years later, Cheng often says how lucky he was and that "half of my achievements belong to her".

After the wedding, Chen Jia-jian went back to the primary school where she had worked, and voluntarily worked as the principal as well as a teacher. She loved students and her work was excellent. On vacations, she always accompanied Cheng to catch frogs for experiments. At night, she escorted him to the laboratory to do experiments or to prepare the lectures. After they got back home, she often cooked midnight snacks. Because Cheng was so busy, Chen Jia-jian helped him by going to see his grandma several times every month. Cheng's grandma also liked her virtuous grand-daughter-in-law.

The University alloted them a professor's lodge which consisted of three stories and a basement. The first floor included a kitchen, dining room, a parlour, a study and a playroom; on the second floor were the bedrooms of different sizes. The third floor was for storage. The basement was used for keeping grain and firewood.

The lodge was built on a slope near the top of a hill. From the top, Cheng could see Mawei port in the far distance. They often invited students of the biology department to their home to enjoy music and to hold parties at weekends when Chen Jia-jian would cook some cookies to entertain them. Whenever the students had difficulties, the couple always tried their best to help them out. More than half a century has passed, and those students still keep in touch.

* * * * * *

After the war against Japan started in 1937, as a result of the resistance policy taken by the Kuomintang government, soon after the losses of Shanghai and Nanjing, Wuhan, a large city in central China, was lost in October 1938. The Kuomintang government had to move its capital to Chongqing, a mountain city in the south west of the country. Under the threat of attack by the Japanese army, Fujian Christian University decided to move to Shaowu. At that time there were about 1000 students and several hundred staff and their families, and it was not easy to organize such a big move. Most people could only take necessary clothes with them and they travelled to Shaowu carrying their possessions on their shoulders. When they arrived there were not enough houses available. As well as some houses borrowed from the church, the staff had to build simple log cabins by themselves. Finally everyone was settled and teaching began.

Shaowu is a county in the remote north west of Fujian province, in the upper reaches of Fuchunxi river which is one of the three main tributaries of the Min. The old county town has a long history. It is situated in the arms of the Wuyi mountains and surrounded by the rolling hills. There are a lot of resources and scientific secrets hidden in the dense forests of the green and luxuriant mountains, in the murmuring streams and in the hinterlands of Wuyi mountains. Many rare species of animals and plants live in this area, such as horned frogs, monkeys called 'Jiaoshou' by the ancients, salamanders which look like leeches with four legs, bee-eaters, pig-tail rodents, red deer and rare bamboos.

The Wuyi mountains are in an overlapping area of

two zoogeographical realms, the Palearctic and the Oriental. Climate conditions and habitats vary with the altitude. It was an area in which many new species of vertebrates and insects had been found. It was therefore called 'the key area' in which to study the distribution of Chinese animals.

The rolling hills of Wuyi mountains tower into the clouds. The summit of Huanggangshan is 2157 metres above sea level and is a natural boundary of animal distribution. Many species of birds either in the north or in the south cross the mountains to migrate southward or northward every year. During migration, a large number would stay here for a period which made Wuyi mountains a real paradise of birds.

In the dense forest of the Wuyi mountains there is a small village named Guadun. Cheng Tso-hsin knew the village through reading a book on Chinese birds written by Mr La Touche, who had collected many speciemens in Guadun in the 1920s.

On arrival at Shaowu, Cheng asked about the location of Guadun. But as this area had been very hard to reach in the past, nobody knew the village. When Cheng went to the county town he thought that perhaps the county magistrate might know Guadun because it was in his territory. But when he met him he was disappointed: the head of the county had never heard of the village before.

Cheng's next thought was to go to the church. He asked a foreign missionary who had obtained a lot of specimens if he had heard of Guadum. The missionary said yes. "Do you also want to go to Guadun?" he asked. "It really is a haven of peace, a wonderful place! We always have someone going to or coming back from there on Sundays. If you want to visit the village, please follow us!"

Cheng thought that "it is a village of China. As a Chinese, should I follow a guide from another country? Can't I find it by myself?" He thanked the missionary and refused his offer. He decided to look for Guadun by himself.

In the summer holiday of 1939, Fujian Christian University organized a party to visit Guadun consisting of five members and the chairman of the biology department, Prof Cheng Tso-hsin who was to be the leader. They set out on 14 June, following a mountain path to the northwest. On the journey there were high mountains and dense forests, murmuring streams and the continuous calls of partridges and

63

francolins. Having crossed Yangmei and Wangzhu mountains, the party reached Huangkeng village in the afternoon. Since leaving Shaowu they had travelled 40 km. Their arms were burned by the hot sun and their feet were sore from the long walk.

Huangkeng was a large village, surrounded by a long block-house and a deep trench outside with men guarding the entrance and exit. Up the hill there were also block-houses and trenches built by the Kuomintang army when they had fought with the Communists several years previously. Cheng and his party stayed in the village overnight. The second day, having walked for 20 km, they arrived at another village called Dazhulan. There were a few villagers there and most families were very poor. Their houses were simple, mostly covered with bamboo and the bark of trees on the roofs. When they arrived at Dazhulan, the weather quickly turned worse. In the following days it rained very hard and they had to stay there until 21 June, when the rain stopped. They then continued on their way to Guadun.

Three hours later, they arrived at Guadun situated in a valley of Wuyi mountains with a perimeter of about 30 km and divided into three parts, upper, middle and lower Guadun. Each part was occupied by a few families. The majority of the residents were from Fu families (Fu is a surname in Chinese). The residents lived on planting tea and digging bamboo shoots. Their houses were built of wood and bamboo, with two stories. One room on the upper floor was used for storing tea leaves which were dried by a fire made on the first floor. In front of the houses were bamboo mats used not for rest or drying clothes but for drying the tea leaves. In the lower part of Guadun there was a classroom, unused for many years so that it was in bad condition. Apart from the wasted classroom and the simple houses, the scenery of Guadun was really beautiful, rolling hills surrounding the village, the streams swift and clean, flocks of birds singing and calling in the forest. What an unharmonious comparison between such beauty and the old and poor houses in Guadun! As the first Chinese biologist to visit Guadun, what Cheng had gained was not just the great impression of the richness of biological resources and the beauty of the surroundings, but the experience of actually finding and reaching it which he would never forget.

At that time there was a church in Guadun, the

Western-style building towering above the village and dominating it. The blue-eyed missionaries went in and out of Guadun freely, spreading their economic and cultural influences into even the remotest and poorest villages in China. Cheng, very surprised to discover that all the residents in the village were Catholics and had been for three generations, was very upset. He felt that science could not be developed if the country was not reformed.

They left Guadun and walked another five km before arriving at Sangang village, 400 meters lower in altitude than Guadun and on the main road connecting Fujian and Jiangxi provinces, seven km northwest of the village. This is the Tongmu Pass which must be crossed to get to Qianshan county of Jiangxi province.

On 23 June the party left Sangang and, after crossing the Zhuzai mountain, arrived at Longdu. The wooden bridge had been destroyed by the flood so that they had to rebuild it with bamboo; it took them two hours to cross the river. The mountain path was rugged although walking in the shade of dense forests they felt cool. They passed through several small villages such as Gaoqiao and Piken before arriving at

Huangzhuao. The mountains became steeper and it was not easy to climb them. It rained all of a sudden and they had to shelter in a house. They bathed in the stream to refresh themselves and stayed in the village overnight.

The next day, the sun was scorching. Despite the sweltering heat, they encouraged each other and soon arrived at Caodun and then Xingcun at lunch time. After lunch they visited several scenic places on the Wuyi mountains and lodged at the Tianxin Temple at night. The next morning they returned to Xingcun and took a raft to follow the famous Jiuqu stream, returning to Shaowu by bus. It was almost 9 o'clock at night when they arrived at the university. The visit to Guadun was described by Cheng in an article entitled A tour to Guadun which was published in *Science*, the magazine of the Chinese Scientific Society in 1941.

Whilst based in Shaowu, Cheng often led some students to the mountains in the early morning when the birds were most active. They surveyed the whole area once or twice a week and spent several hours in the field each time, recording the species of birds they found, investigating the status of migration, studying the breeding biology and monitoring the population

67

dynamics. This work took about three years and the results were published in Census of Birds of Shaowu District for three years (1938-41) which appeared in *Biological Bulletin*, a scientific journal of Fujian Christian University. It was the first scientific paper based on field studies of the species and ecology of wild birds. In it Cheng presented the results of bird species in Shaowu, the staying period and the distribution and numbers of each species. This paper attracted much attention from the circle of science and won a first-class award from the ministry of education. It was also one of Cheng's first real results in the field of bird studies. He realised that it was only a beginning and there was much more work to be done. Although there were many difficulties to be overcome, he made up his mind to work harder in order to realize his wish that Chinese resources should be studied mainly by Chinese scientists.

Dr Cheng as a visiting professor in America (1945-46)

BACK TO AMERICA

After Cheng Tso-hsin moved to Shaowu with Fujian Christian University in 1938, he was recommended by the professor committee to be the dean of studies while still continuing his scientific research and teaching. On the right hand side of his desk were placed what materials he needed for teaching and on the left the materials he used to study birds. He would spend one or two evenings every week going to ordinary people's houses to promote knowledge of popular science.

In 1943 the dean of students, Lin Guan-de, became seriously ill and had to stay at home to recuperate. The president, Lin Jin-run, asked Cheng to act concurrently as the dean of students. Usually the task of admonishing students was the responsibility of the Kuomingtang secretary, but Cheng was not a party member. Nevertheless the president insisted on his taking the post (in name only) temporarily. The president also encouraged him to join the Kuomingtang, as it would benefit him and the school. But Cheng wasn't interested in politics, only in contributing wholeheartedly to saving the nation by science. He believed in keeping aloof from politics and material pursuits and did not know that in the old society all intellectuals served the dominant classes. This nominal extra duty brought him much trouble in later years.

In 1944 the culture departments of China and America agreed to exchange several professors to improve academic communication. The Chinese party comprised Yan Jici (research fellow in the Institute of Physics, Peking Academy of Sciences) and Mei Yiqi (the president of Yanjing University). The universities in Shanghai and north-west China could respectivly recommend one person, and Fujian Christian University could also send someone. Many people at Fujian Christian University wanted to go so the president asked the professor committee to vote and Cheng was selected.

At that time, Fujian Christian University was situated in the mountain area of north west Fujian, because of occupation by the Japanese army and railways, cars and ships were not available to the public. Communications were very difficult. The Kuomingtang government was based in Chongqing

71

and the procedures for going abroad had to be dealt with there. To get from Shaowu to Chongqing, involved a dangerous detour by plane.

If Cheng Tso-hsin went abroad, Jia-jian had to face all the problems he left behind. Their fourth child had just been born while at the same time, Cheng's younger brothers, sisters and cousins (grandma had died after moving to Shaowu) and Jia-jian's sisters and younger brother moved to Shaowu one after another. They were responsible for taking care of two big families. But Cheng thought that the chance was precious, and insisted on accepting the invitation. As a virtuous wife, Jia-jian understood and, although worried, agreed he should go.

In April 1945, Cheng set out from Shaowu and went first to Zhangdin county in Fujian by car. He transferred to a plane to Kunming and then to Chongqin. After going through formalities, they finally left by air, by way of India, Iran, Egypt and Morocco. They then crossed the Atlantic and, having gone in a big circle, finally reached Washington. The total time was two months.

Cheng communicated with more than ten universities and museums on the eastern seaboard of

America, making academic reports or introducing Chinese education to the universities, or examining Chinese bird specimens in every museum, especially type specimens and relevant research literature.

He also acted as a visiting professor. His research into ornithology received special attention among academic groups. The American government gave him a professor's allowance, so his living conditions were excellent. But there was no way to send money home, and he could not receive a letter from his family either. Cheng did not know how Jia-jian could keep such a large family in war-time circumstances and he kept worrying about them.

With news of the end of the Second World War, as well as the Chinese war of resistance against Japan, Cheng was faced once again with a difficult decision. His old school, University of Michigan, invited him to undertake post-doctorate research. But he declined, thinking that his country had undergone eight years of a war of resistance and it had been a disastrous period. Everything was just waiting to be rebuilt and he felt that he should devote himself to China.

Before long he heard from Jia-jian and learned that Fujian Christian University had moved back to

73

Fuzhou. Old and young in the family were safe and sound. He could not stay in America any longer and so he politely declined the American invitation to stay and prepared to return to China. At the same time, Cheng received invitations from the Guangzhou Linnan University and the Zhongshan Medical College but he thought that as he had been recommended by the Fujian Christian University to go abroad, he should return there. In September 1946 he returned to Fujian Christian University and resumed his post.

Cheng brought a great deal of luggage back from America, large quantities of which were relevant to records of Chinese bird species. There were several boxes of literature and notebooks. After returning to school, he lost no time in sorting them out after work.

Prof and Mrs Cheng on the campus of Fujian Christian University, Fuzhou, Fujian (1946)

75

THE CHINESE BIRDS LIST
AND THE REVOLUTION

A history of Chinese bird-study was not available. In ancient books there were plenty of records of birds. According to archeologists in the Shang dynasty (c 15th-11th century BC), there were birds' names in Jiaguwen. In the Han dynasty, Shushen listed 40 species of birds in *Shuo Wen Jie Zi;* Er Ya listed 78 groups of birds in the spring and autumn, each group a king of bird, but also one group referring to several kinds. By the Ming dynasty, in *Compendium of Materia Medica,* Li Shi-zhen mentions 77 kinds of birds. In addition, some birds' names appeared in *Shi Mimg* and *Ji Jie.* After the Ming dynasty, Chinese biology gradually declined.

Because the Chinese had not put aside any resources for bird research, foreigners seized the opportunity to come and help. After the Opium War, at the time of military, political and economic invasion, the Imperialist invasion of Chinese culture intensified and they sent specialists to look for Chinese birds. In 1863 the Englishman Swinhoe wrote the first Chinese Bird List, in which 454 bird species were recorded. In 1884 the Frenchmen David and Oustalet also published a monograph of Chinese birds, in which the numbers of bird species had gone up to 807. From 1926 to 1927 the foreigners Gee, Moffett and Wilder together compiled *A Tentative List of Chinese Birds* and then in 1931 Gee replenished and revised it and listed 1093 species and 575 subspecies, 1668 species and subspecies in total. But among species and subspecies in this list there were more than 200 species about which there are doubts and should be deleted.

Our birds are famous all over the world. For Cheng Tso-hsin, as a Chinese scholar, it was a duty to make them known to the public. But it was very difficult to undertake the research. First, there were no funds for him to conduct his research throughout China. The Kuomingtang were preparing to redouble military expenditure so there were no funds for science;the American church only helped some aspects of education, which weren't even sufficient to pay for administration of the school, to say nothing of carrying out scientific research.

Furthermore the Chinese social order was in chaos

and transport was disorganised. If he wanted to go to museums in England, America, Germany or USSR to do research on bird species of our country, it was nearly impossible. Chinese scientists have moral integrity, even under such difficult circumstances and Cheng swore to adhere to his chosen course. He took all his spare time to go on field trips in Fujian; he compared the specimens examined in America, jobs which were very difficult and complicated.

In order to distinguish subtle differences between bird specimens, he would have to devote his heart and soul to research for a long time, which was easier said than done. At that time, Cheng already had no free time or holiday, and no time to undertake even a little housework. He put his whole body and mind to work.

In the March 1945 *Journal* of Fujian Christian University Biology Institute there was a report on Cheng's working conditions at that time. Since Dr Cheng was dean of studies, he has had to undertake the important role of promoting academic work. He was busy all the time, and had no time to rest. He went to his office to do administration as soon as he got up; he went to the science hall and researched with undivided attention the whole afternoon, and wrote

78

books at night. He didn't waste a minute or even a second. This is something which was not lost on the students and which was an example to them.

After many long nights in 1947 he published *A Checklist of Chinese Birds* in the Transections of the Chinese Association for the Advancement of Sciences. In this publication he listed 1087 species and 912 subspecies of Chinese birds, totalling 1999 forms, an increase of 331 over Gee, Moffett and Wilder's *Tentative List of Chinese Birds.* At the same time, he made extensive corrections to the scientifc names of birds. It was the first checklist of China's birds published by a Chinese scholar. Its publication symbolized that Chinese ornithological research had reached a new level. The book also provided a basis for further research on the birds of our country after the founding of the People's Republic of China.

* * * * * *

In 1946, the Kuomingtang attacked the area liberated by the communists which caused the outbreak of the Civil War. In 1947 because of government corruption inflation was serious. People had no means of making a livelihood; anti-fatigue, anti-civil war, anti-persecuting demonstrations took place everywhere on a considerable scale in the Kuomingtang-controlled area. Although the authorities had prohibited students from taking part in the parades many times, they were not successful.

Students in Fujian Christian University, ignoring the authority's prohibitions, took part in demonstrations throughout the city. Cheng Tso-hsin was blamed for not being strict with them. Cheng Xien, the president of that time, had been to America. The school's trustees chose the principal of a theological college to take his place. The students went on strike to show their discontent. The new president asked Cheng to persuade students to resume their studies. Cheng realized that things had got out of hand so much that research was impossible, so he made up his mind to leave Fujian Christian University. He went to Nanjing city on the pretext of asking for leave.

Cheng had a deep affection for Fujian Christian University, where he had studied and worked for 20 years. He had dedicated his youth to this university and had spent a memorable time there during his career. But the situation became serious: he had to depart so quickly that he had to leave his sons and daughters in the care of his retired father.

When his students discovered this, they gathered on the wharf to see him off, some even hiring a motorboat to follow the steamer, waving to wish their teacher and master a favourable wind and speedy return to the school.

Cheng worked as a senior editor in Nanjing, helped by his considerable experience in writing books and the publication of many scientific papers over the previous years. He was appointed a professor at Central University (today's Nanjing University) shortly afterwards. At the same time, he was able to carry on some research work on birds. Before long, Jia-jing also went to Nanjian with their four children and the family lived together once again.

Inflation was a serious problem and, because Cheng's salary could not support the family, Jia-jian got a job as assistant editor. At the end of 1948, politically-active people in Nanjing moved to Taiwan, one after another, and the director of the Institute also advised Cheng to move there. Cheng faced a major decision for the second time.

He was deeply disappointed at the behaviour of the Kuomingtang, but he knew little about the Communist Party. He was neither a landlord nor a capitalist so he had nothing to share. What concerned him most was whether or not the Communist Party supported scientists and science. He went to talk to a man in the Institute who was believed to be the most progessive person. It was not until Nanjing's liberation that he was known to be a member of the secret Chinese Communist Party. He told Cheng "the communist party does need science and many scientists." Cheng asked him about the ornithologists. The answer was "certainly, it needs all kinds of scientists and technicians in every field of activity."

After this, Cheng was reassured and decided to stay in Nanjing to await its liberation. When his superior brought him the plane tickets, he firmly declined them. It was an important choice in his life and it is because of it he achieved so much in his research work. He subsequently became a member of the Chinese Communist Party. Today he is confident that he made the correct decision.

Cheng longed for a powerful China established in the world and after Nanjing's liberation he saw the dawn. He celebrated the liberation with the people of Nanjing; some members of the Institute went to Taiwan and others remained. Society had changed greatly and everything was so fresh.

The Military Control Commission assigned agents to organize members of the Institute to learn Chairman Mao's *On the People's Democracy Dictatorship*, *On New Democracism*, Ai Siqi's *Public Philsophy*. After that everyone began to understand the revolution. Jia-jian also helped in the work of the Nanjing Women's Union in June 1949. The only thing they worried about was their four children. When they heard that the PLA had decided to make a forced crossing of the Yangzi river, they sent their children to Fuzhou for fear that they could not be able to stand the hardships of war.

As the new China was born, the students' autonomous association and the school's administration board at Fujian Christian University telegraphed Cheng to ask him to return to Fuzhou to take up a teaching position. Even his father in Fuzhou sent an urgent message. The new president of Fujian Christian University, Yang Chang-doing, even went to Nanjing and Cheng was greatly moved.

83

Preparatory committee of the National Museum of Natural History in April 1950. Professor Cheng is second from the left.

Key to map opposite

Solid lines showing multi-disciplied exploitations sponsored by the Academy of Sciences.
Broken lines indicating expeditions on birds taken by the Institute of Zoology.

1.   Insect-eating irds in Chang-li orchard district in
      Hobei Province (1953-56).
2.   Southern parts of Yunnan province (1955-59).
3.   Dislocating of water from the south northward
      area (1957-60).
4.   Meridional Himalayas (1958-80).
5.   Southern parts of Xizang (Tibet) (1959).
6.   Qin-Ba mountainous region (1956-65).
7.   Southern regions of Xinjiang (1958-60).
8.   Hubei and Hunan hilly regions (1959-60).
9.   Hainan Is. (now a province) (1960-74).
10.   Three northern afforestation areas (1970-72).

There are a number of minor expeditions taken in southern Henan, southern Shantung, and northwestern Fujian.

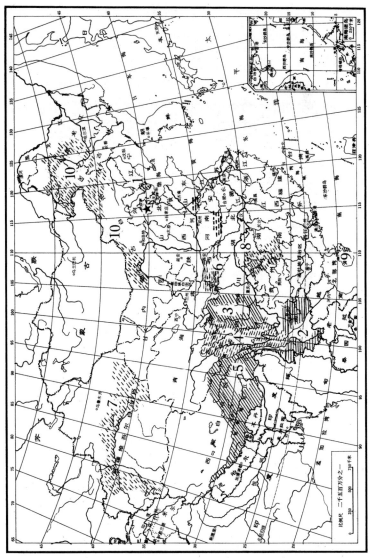

Map showing field explorations sponsored by the Chinese Academy of Sciences.

85

But he was being successful in his research work and enjoyed considerable prestige both in China and abroad. The Chinese Communist Party believed in him and required him to make an even greater contribution. One day in 1950, after being consulted about his work, he was told that there was a new post for him with the compiling and publishing commission of the Chinese Academy of Sciences and he went to Beijing in very high spirits.

Shortly after arriving in Beijing he met Cheng Hong, a former student of Fujian Christian University who was a close friend of Jia-jian's elder sister. She had left Fujian Christian University to plunge into the revolution but then followed the Long March. Due to fear of implicating good friends, she had not dared tell Jia-jian's elder sister. At that time, she was a doctor at the Central Garrison Regiment. When she learned that Jia-jian was still in Nanjing, she recommended her to work in the National Women's Union. Before long, Jia-jian and their children went to Beijing one after another. They began a new life.

BIRD RESEARCHES

In spring 1955 Zhang Tian-shan, a reporter of the *Guangming Daily,* came to Fenghuang mountain to interview Cheng Tso-hsin and he wrote a report entitled At the foot of Fenghuang Mountain. In 1956, Yao Feng-zao, a reporter of the *People's Daily*, also went there and interviewed Cheng Tso-hsin and then wrote a long report entitled The Secret of a Tit Egg, which was published in *Wenhui Daily* on 6 October 1956. Cheng's hard work on bird research was vividly described in the article of which the following are some excerpts.

Prof Cheng said "They had begun to investigate birds in Changli in 1953. In the first year they carried guns and walked all around the fruit tree areas, collecting nearly 200 species of birds. In the second year, they observed the life cycles and habits of these through a telescope. The dissection of their stomachs was carried out by the Department of Entomology in order to make clear which ones ate pests and benefitted the fruit trees. At the same time, they hung more than 200 artificial nestboxes in the orchard to

87

attract useful birds.

"The results of the investigations and research of the previous two years showed that the great tit was the most common beneficial bird for the fruit trees. With a short breeding cycle, they ate lots of pests and were permanent residents in Changli. We hung up nestboxes there last year and, as a result, there were seven nestboxes in which they nested, layed eggs and hatched all their chicks.

"He also took me to see the nestboxes hanging in the trees, which looked like postboxes, though a little smaller, and there was a round hole for the bird to go in and out. When we reached the neighbourhood of a village, there was a nestbox hung in a pear tree in the yard of a peasant's house. One of Cheng's assistants told us, 'The old grandpa of this house did not know what they had hung it for but when we told him it was for attracting 'cipou' (means great tit) to eat pests, he didn't believe it at first, but when we gave him a telescope and told him to look himself he, as expected, told us that he saw 'cipou' were eating pests. In a short while, he took down the nestbox and hung it on the tree inside his own yard!'

"When we reached box ten, they excitedly told us,

'it was first nestbox that tits resided in. They nested, layed eggs and hatched their young. Everyone was so excited that all of us rushed to box ten. Since this was the first tit to live in a box, other boxes must also have been occupied.'

"It was said since they had found a nest in box ten, they had got up to observe before half past four every morning and did not return until there was no noise in the nestbox. They persisted in watching them like this until their chicks had flown. Not only were the times and species of pests observed, but also the hatching and rate of growth by climbing the tree and opening the nestbox. Within five minutes they had to climb up and down so as not to disturb the parents. This was repeated several times a day. Cheng said, 'We will continue our work this year in order to find out whether it affects the output of the fruit trees. Furthermore we will move a bird's nest. At present, there are few great tits in many orchards, we will move nests to orchards and observe whether they are willing to move with them. This experiment is very important, but it will take a long time to finish."

In addition, Cheng told the reporter a story of an odd egg. One morning they had found an odd egg in the nestbox no. 116. Tits' eggs were usually oval, but this one was somewhat pointed, which aroused much interest: Would it hatch out? If so, what would the product look like? Early next morning he climbed the pear tree to the nest. But to his surprise the egg had gone.

A little disappointed he climbed down. He went to another tree 50 meters away in low spirits and sat down and, with leaves hiding his body, concentrated on looking at nestbox no. 116. It was the first phenomenon he had met in his work on birds for decades. Where had the egg gone? Could someone have stolen it? Maybe children of the Fenghuang mountain had frightened the tit away and removed the eggs; perhaps it had been eaten by snakes? A few days previously he and his assistants had removed a snake from a cave and thus saved a brood of young woodpeckers. But something was going into nextbox no. 116 and quickly he picked up the telescope to see what it was. Suddenly, a sparrow flew out from the small opening holding a tit's egg in it's mouth and then a female followed it out.

The secret was clear; the sparrow had stolen the tit's egg, which aroused Cheng's interest once again.

Hanging nest boxes in hilly forests at Lou-Shan, Henan province (1970).

He would continue his observations to discover why sparrows steal tits' eggs and how tits deal with them. The pair of sparrows returned as expected, but this time they carried in their mouths not the tit's egg but feathers and twigs and they took over box no. 116 from the tits.

The tits soon returned, protesting "cipou, cipou", but they dared not get too close to the sparrows. They seemed to be afraid of them because they were not strong enough to compete. Cheng was angry but also amused. With the secret resolved, it was time for him to go back for a rest, but he remained there for nearly half a day, mourning for the tits. This research proved to be very important to China as we shall see. Next morning he brought his gun to kill the sparrows. The tits returned to their nest. But the odd shape of the tits' egg remained unsolved.

* * * * * *

In the winter of 1955 there was a nationwide movement to eliminate 'four pests': sparrows, mice, flies and mosquitoes. Old and young, men and women all took part: students left their classes, cardres stopped their office work and thus, all through Beijing there was the deafening sound of gongs and drums, driving sparrows from their nests until they were exhausted and fell to their deaths. In open areas, nets and poisoned baits were used. After three day's continuous noise in Beijing almost all sparrows had died.

The following year, the China Zoological Society held its second national convention at Qingdao, Shan Dong province. The problem of sparrows was raised.

Some claimed that sparrows ate so much cereal that they were called "house thieves" and that in the vast rural areas, "there were tens of thousands of sparrows and should be killed". On the other hand, someone said sparrows liked to eat insects and they should not be killed. Many different opinions were voiced and the debate became intense.

Evidence from other countries was cited: it was said that in the last century, France had made an order to eradicate sparrows. Six shillings could be obtained if one sparrow was killed, so everyone had set out to kill them. Several years later it was realised that not only had it cost the government a lot of money but it had also caused a severe plague of insects in fruit trees which, in turn, reduced production significantly. So the government had cancelled the order. As the Secretary-General of the China Zoological Society, Cheng had to express his opinion. It was that the sparrow could not be eliminated in any case because of its world-wide distribution. Furthermore sparrows should not be eradicated but the damage they did should be reduced and brought under control. Sparrows live on insects while they raise their young, which is beneficial to human beings. Members taking part in the meeting thus concluded that not enough research had been done on the sparrow, a bird which is so close to the economy and life of human beings.

After the meeting, Cheng and his colleagues collected 848 sparrow specimens in Changli, where fruit trees were planted, and the agriculturial regions in the suburbs of Beijing. They made an extensive study of sparrow food for an entire year, mainly by dissecting their crops and stomachs but also by observation in the gathering areas. They measured the percentages of all the contents. In sparrows, as with other small birds, the volume of stomach content is small and not easy to weigh. So the method of water level replacement was adopted. They also sorted out the various different foods so that comparisions could be made. In addition experiments were carried out on captive bred birds and although the findings differed greatly from those from the wild, the results could be used as a basis for evaluation.

Cheng and his assistants published their paper Primary report of sparrow's food in the *Journal of Zoology* in 1957. Based on their results, they also wrote articles on the good and harm sparrows do in the *People's Daily* and other newspapers. His investigations showed that "In winter, sparrows mostly live on grass seeds; in spring, when laying, hatching and raising the young, a great number of insects and their eggs are consumed. In young birds, insect eggs make up 95 percent of their food; during July and August, during harvest, sparrows harm crops and places for storing grain. After harvest, they mainly eat the leftovers of crops in the fields and grass seeds. Therefore, during the period of hatching, sparrows are beneficial to us, and they do harm both to the harvest area and storing places; in woods, cities and in other seasons, they should be left alone. We should be very clear about what harm sparrows cause, deal with it according to different regions, different seasons and different environments". Cheng persisted with this scientific approach while all over the country people were occupied with the noise of eradicating sparrows.

The opinions of the scientists were appreciated by the Chinese government. At the time of revising the draft Outline of Agriculture Development, it pointed out, "sparrows may not be eliminated in cities and wooded areas." When the Outline was formally passed in 1959, bugs replaced sparrows as one of the 'four pests'. The pathetic sparrows should thus appreciate Professor Cheng Tso-hsin for acting as their 'attorney' and protecting them.

It was unforseen that his work to rehabilitate sparrows was later regarded as a heinous crime in the Cultural Revolution. Someone said Cheng used sparrows to stand against the great leader, Chairman Mao and he underwent severe criticism. At one of these meetings, someone scolded Cheng, "do you know what crime you committed?" Cheng thinking that he had made no mistake, replied, "I don't know." The critics responded angrily "you! the reactionary academic, dare to praise the sparrow and oppose the highest instructions!"

Cheng could not understand, despite much reflection. Sparrows were still eating pests! Moreover, they had been replaced by bugs in the Outline of Agriculture Development. Why did they attack him like this? Later, someone told Cheng secretly that the *Highest Instructions*, printed by Hong Wei Guard of the Chinese Academy of Sciences stated: "Sparrows should not be killed any more and were to be replaced by bugs..." Cheng was delighted.

It was adopted in section 11 of the textbook of the

full-time primary school in 1988, under the title of Rehabilitating the Sparrows. One passage says that "at that time, quite a few people agreed with Cheng Tso-hsin, but no one dared to voice their opinions because 'eliminating the sparrows' was the instruction of Chairman Mao and the Central Committee of the Party. But Cheng was different from others. He believed in scientific truth and held that Chairman Mao and the Central Committee must in the end believe the truth of science. He thought it was a sacred duty for a scientist to explore, pursue and propagate the truth. He published his research results and opinions openly, ignorant of his personal gain and loss. At the end of the text, he wrote, "The 'unjust verdict' for sparrows was thus 'reversed'. Everyone praised Cheng for his unselfish scientific approach and extoled him as a scientist of integrity."

* * * * * *

The red junglefowl is the ancestor of the domestic chicken. However Charles Darwin, the British naturalist, wrote in *Variation in Domestic Animals and Plants* that the ancestor of the Chinese domestic

97

chicken was not from China, but from India. Because this point of view came from Darwin's book no one doubted it, but Cheng Tso-hsin did not agree. He led a party of young colleagues on an expedition to the southern areas of Yunan province to try finding which species is the true ancestor of the Chinese chicken.

One day, after sunset, they were returning slowly with cameras on shoulders and guns in hands when suddenly two red junglefowl appeared in a field about 300 m ahead of them. The red junglefowl looked quite similar to a domestic chicken. The rust-brown hen walked quickly in front; a chestnut-red cock followed her. Feathers on the crown and nape are sickle-shaped, glowing with metallic reflection. Its tail feathers are long and droop low with the central rectrices the colour of glowing metallic-green.

The red junglefowl has very sensitive sight and hearing, and it is also very shy of human beings. Alarmed, the hen jumped down from the branch of a tree and quickly ran into the undergrowth with her tail feathers hanging down. The cock, seemingly with no time to escape, flew away. At that moment Cheng's colleague fired and the cock was shot. They ran to the place where it had fallen with great enthusiasm

98

because it was a valuable species for scientific research. Unfortunately, after much searching, they could not find it in the thick vegetation. Although Cheng had observed so many wild birds on his trip to Yunnan such as thrushes, weavers, sunbirds, hornbills and green peafowls, none of them was of any use to this investigation to clarify whether or not the red junglefowl was the ancestor of the Chinese domestic chicken.

The idea that the Chinese domestic chicken was imported from India can be found in several books of poultry biology published in Japan, China and the countries of Europe and in America. All of them are based on Darwin's *Variation in Domestic Animals and Plants* in which he wrote, "In India, the domestication of the wild red junglefowl was at the time when the book *Institutes of Manu* had been completed, about 1,200 BC". He also wrote "The domestic chicken is one of the poultry of Western countries, and it was introduced to China in a dynasty around 1,400 BC." Here the "Western country" is India.

Why couldn't the Chinese chicken be a domesticated Chinese red junglefowl? Isn't it too complicated to introduce it into China after it had been domesticated in India, rather than Chinese people domesticating it by themselves using local wild stock? These were the questions Cheng posed.

The weather changed quickly. It became cloudy and windy while Cheng and his colleagues continued to look for the shot red junglefowl. Black clouds covered the sky above the forest, the branches of the trees swayed, and the wind whistled. They could not continue their search and had to run for shelter. There were many trees with thick vegetation which, like a huge umbrella, provided a refuge for them. Rain fell with lightning, accompanied by thunder. They could only see the white sheets of rain like a huge book in front of them. Then some sentences of Darwin's work occurred to Cheng. He remembered clearly that Darwin had written that he made his conclusion of the ancestor of Chinese chicken according to the *Chinese Encyclopedia*.

What was the *Chinese Encyclopedia*? During which dynasty had it been published? Who was the author? Darwin did not give these details. He had only mentioned that the book was published in the year of 1596. Cheng found out that *Compendium of Materia Medica* was published by Li Shizhen, a distinctive naturalist and doctor, in 1596. But he did not mention the ancestor of the Chinese chicken in his book.

In another place Darwin said that the *Chinese Encyclopedia* was printed in 1609. Cheng searched among the classical books again and found that *Three Talents Pictorial Serial Books* was the only important book which had been published that year. In it there is a paragraph which says "There are many kinds of chickens which occur in each area of Shu, Lu, Jin and Yue. Yue's is smaller and Shu's is bigger, Lu's chicken is the largest. According to the myth, the chicken lives in the sun. The chicken lived originally in the West, when the sun arose from the eastern side, the chicken flew into it." The West mentioned here obviously represents the western areas of China, places such as Shu or Jin, not India which is west of China. This made Cheng doubt Darwin's conclusions.

After several days of research Cheng and his colleagues found 16 scattered junglefowl looking for food near a valley of a mountain village. The junglefowl behaved like domestic chickens, removing fallen leaves and topsoil with their feet and bills, and looking for worms, seeds and the roots of bamboo shoots. Sometimes they dug quite a hole in the ground. Cheng and his colleagues were very excited at their discovery. Through continuous observation they found some of the junglefowl would move into the mountain village and join up with the local domestic chickens. They ate together and sometimes mated with them.

One night, about three or four o'clock in the early morning, Cheng and his colleagues were awoken by strange calls. "Erer.er----er." Cheng rose and listened to them carefully. His colleagues did not think it was a chicken calling, so what was it? Their host told them that it was a Chahua chicken.

Chahua chicken is the local name of the red junglefowl. The name comes from its calls, which sound like a sentence in Chinese 'Cha Hua Liang Duo' (it means, in local dialect, two flowers of the Camelia). Listening to the rhythmical calls excited Cheng. He felt he was hearing the 'Chahua' chicken declaring its right of existence in Chinese lands. It seemed that they were declaring they were the descendants of the Chinese ancestor.

According to the results of on-the-spot scientific research, Cheng concluded that it was Darwin's oversight that misinterpreted the Western areas of

China as India. Many authors of poultry biology treated Darwin's words as true and consequently they echoed the wrong views one by one.

'Daming' was the title of an emperor's reign, which represented that of the Emperor Xiao-Wu, during the South-North Dynasty, about 420-479 AD. The author of *Three Talents Pictorial Serial Books* considered that during this period the domestic chicken was introduced to the east from the western areas of China. However, this argument was untenable, since as early as 770 -721 BC, raising chickens was very popular in China. The King of Wu, Fu Chai, had built three coops for raising chickens, each of them about 1 km^2. Later, the King of Yue, Gou Jian, had also raised a large number of chickens. In the time of Qin and Han Dynasty, raising chickens was very common at the lower reaches of the Yangtze river, just as was described in the poem, 'Chicken calls near a small inn in the moon shine, the floor of the bridge was covered by the frost'. Some others thought that 'Daming' is not the title of an emperor's reign but means the sun. There was a legend that 'There is a chicken in the sun and a rabbit in the moon', so 'Daming' rises in the east and the chicken flies into it.

This point of view is out of the legend and is a type of feudal superstition. In the research work on the ancestry of the Chinese domestic chicken, Cheng Tso-hsin expanded his research area to the relics of the prehistoric age. A potsherd with a shape of chicken indicated that the domestic chicken must have existed before the potsherd. Cheng's textual research was confined to existing historical materials.

Chickens had been recorded by inscription on bones and tortoise shell as early as *Institutes of Manu.* So Cheng concluded that Chinese chickens were domesticated by Chinese people, not introduced from India. The ancestor of the Chinese chicken is the red junglefowl living in China, not India's junglefowl. Although he respected Darwin's achievements, Cheng corrected the wrong conclusions with pleasure.

* * * * * *

In the spring of 1960 Cheng Tso-hsin climbed mount Emei in Sichuan province. 'The most beautiful mountain in the world', it is also one of the four famous Buddhist mountains. The endless mountains, flowering trees, warm climate and beautiful landscape

104

attract hundreds of thousands of tourists all the year around and the many animals and plants in the area attract experts. When Cheng and his colleagues climbed toward the summit they met an experienced hunter, about 60 years old, short, sturdy and below the bushy eyebrows was a pair of sharp, sincere eyes. The hunter invited them into his thatched cottage. It was small and simple and in a corner were some old and blackened cooking utensils. On the walls hung several birds, one of which was very striking.

Cheng examined the specimen carefully, and was dumbfounded: it was a rare cock silver pheasant! Its crown seemed like a splendid cap; behind the red comb there were several strands of blue feathers, glittering like diamonds. The feathers on the underpart were blueblack, creating a sharp contrast with the back and wings. Most significant were the long white rectrices which made its body slender and beautiful.

Cheng knew that the silver pheasant was rare and was protected in China. There were ten sub-species, all of them distributed in the bamboo forests of tropical and subtropical zones in Yunnan, Guangdong, Guangxi and Hainan in China as well as Cambodia, Vietnam, and other parts of south-east Asia. It had never been found in the Emei area in Sichuan province before. He was thus surprised and wondered where it had come from. Had it been released here by tourists? The old hunter also said that this kind of bird was extremly rare and seldom seen; it normally inhabited the forest in the mountainous areas and was very shy. When disturbed, it usually ran up-hill hurriedly, glancing right and left; it did not fly until it reached the summit.

In the following days, Cheng and his colleagues captured several silver pheasants, indicating that it was a native of Emei rather than an introduction from elsewhere. Cheng wondered if the silver pheasant of mount Emei was the same sub-species as those of the south and whether there was any relationship between the silver pheasant here and those of other areas

He returned to Beijing with the silver pheasant specimens he had collected. He put them on his working table to make careful comparisions but could not found any striking differences between them and the southern specimens. Nevertheless he reasoned that since mount Emei was hundreds of miles from the southern region, the remarkable differences in living conditions should lead to variations between the birds.

He turned over the specimen from Emei and carefully examined the plumage from neck to breast, back to underside, and head to rectrices and then he found something strange. The lateral rectrices of this bird were completely black, while those of the southern subspecies were white with thin black streaks, a very significant difference. He also found that there were also other differences in the black streaks on the back, shoulder and wing between the Emei and southern specimens. But because the differences were not obvious they were easy to overlook. Cheng concluded that the Emei silver pheasant was not the same as the silver pheasant of the South. It was a new sub-species and he named it the Emei silver pheasant.

In zoological taxonomy, 'species' is the basic unit. If the animals of the same species live in different areas and have some marked differences between them caused by geographical isolation, they are considered to be a 'sub-species'. Because study of birds has been carried out in Western countries for about 200-300 years, the possibility of finding a new species or sub-species is not very high but in developing countries, such as China, there are many

107

places that remain unexplored, so the possibility is higher. In fact, since the founding of The People's Republic of China, Chinese ornithologists have discovered more than 20 new sub-species of birds, two thirds of them by Cheng. The Emei silver pheasant is a good example.

Cheng and his colleagues subsequently wrote a paper on the discovery and submitted it to *Acta Zootaxonomica Sinica.* After its publication, Cheng sent copies to researchers in the same field, who included Prof Stresemann, the famous German ornithologist. His discovery was soon confirmed in international academic circles.

A year later, Cheng received a letter from Professor Traylor, director of the ornithological section of the Chicago Natural History Museum in the United States who said that, as early as 1930 Mr Smith, an ornithologist of the Museum, had collected specimens in Emei mountains and brought some silver pheasants back to Chicago. Unfortunately, Mr Smith himself had not examined the specimens carefully and did not find any differences between them and those of other areas.

In the 1960s, when Prof Traylor studied the

specimens again, he did find some unique characteristics in the Emei silver pheasant and thought that it was a new sub-species. In order to pay his respects to Cheng for his contribution to Chinese ornithology, Prof Traylor named the 'new' sub-species Cheng's silver pheasant and sent a draft paper to a British ornithological journal. The editor-in-chief of that journal sent it to Prof Stresemann. According to the international rules of zoological nomenclature, since Cheng had discovered the Emei silver pheasant before Prof Traylor, the sub-species should be scientifically called 'Emei silver pheasant', and 'Cheng's silver pheasant' thus became a synonym only.

Sometime later, Prof Stresemann wrote to Cheng humorously that, "At present, the Americans and the Chinese don't agree with each other in many affairs. However, I have found at least one common point that both of you share. It is that both of you think the Emei silver pheasant is a new sub-species. The Chinese found it before the Americans. Please accept my sincere congratulations."

Cheng continued with this line of research, connecting his discovery of the Emei sub-species with the theory of origin and evolution of silver pheasants.

He discovered that among the 14 sub-species of the silver pheasants, half exist in southern Yunnan and the surrounding areas. Theoretically speaking, southern Yunnan is perhaps the centre of its distribution as well as the place of origin. In addition to the Emei sub-species, there are another two sub-species where the cock has black marks on the lateral rectrices, one of them in Hainan, the other in southern Cambodia. As with the Emei sub-species, they were all located in the peripheral region of the silver pheasants' distributional range.

Cheng thought that because the upside of the cock silver pheasant is mainly white, the sub-species with white lateral rectrices are more-developed, and the subspecies with black lateral rectrices are less-developed in the evolutionary scale because they have not turned white. According to its current distribution, the subspecies with the white lateral rectrices are concentrated in southern Yunnan, which is the centre of its distribution, while the ones with black lateral rectrices are scattered in Emei of Sichuan, Hainan island and southern Cambodia where they are at the edge and far from the centre of distribution.

Many biologists traditionally argued that the area where the primitive sub-species was found was the reliable indicator of the place of origin of the species under consideration. But Cheng has an opposing viewpoint. He considered that in the struggle for existence the more-developed sub-species occupies the place where it originated and expels the less-developed sub-species to the periphery where they may remain to be rare or endangered for a time. This competitive expulsion principle is in accord with Darwin's theory of natural selection and offers supplementary evidence in support of the theory of evolution.

PUBLIC CRITICISM

During the unprecedented Great Cultural Revolution, Cheng Tso-hsin did not escape criticism or examination. As with other scholars and specialists, he was given a label of 'reactionary authority' and forced to clean corridors, lavatories and other menial hard work while undergoing unreasonable criticism and endless examination. Cheng and other famous national scholars, such as Tong Di-zhou, Chen Shi-xiang, Liu Cong-le, formed 'a group sentenced to rehabilitation through labour'. Labour was nothing new to those scientists who had had to take part-time work abroad in their early years. They had never regarded labouring as humbling, but doing labour as punishment toward scientists confused them.

At one public meeting of criticism and denouncement, some people took a 'bird' to the platform made from the various parts of different birds. They asked Cheng to identify it. They thought "no matter what you answer, we can attack you and declare that you are a fake, not a real scientist".

Cheng, noted for his meticulous scholarship, never

112

thought that they would do such a shameful thing. Examining the specimen he said formally, "I have never seen such a bird. I don't know what it is." He knew what would follow: the meeting would use his answer "I don't know" as proof that he was not a real scientist or authority. However, as a scientist, he valued the facts and could only respond strictly according to the facts.

At the meeting, someone said in a low voice "He is the real scientist and he has done what a real authority should do". Twenty years later, when people recall the story, few are not moved by his realism. As a scholar, Cheng could never understand why they should seek to deceive him in order to persecute him.

To criticize Cheng and to make him 'notorious', the reactionaries wrote dazibao (large-character posters) which were fabricated to viciously attack him. Facing the criticism, however, Cheng did not keep silent. Being serious about every thing, Cheng did not want to conform to the trend of that age. He used every opportunity to explain his ideas and wrote dazibao to put forward the facts. On one occasion, to shame him, someone produced a pigeon and ordered Cheng to make a specimen of it which is difficult because the pigeon's skin is very thin and difficult to peel off.

Cheng was over 60 years old. His eyesight was not as good as it had been. When he made the specimen, he wondered whether a man studying animal husbandry would have to strip an ox's skin and a man studying wild animals would have to strip a tiger's skin! If he had not felt that research still needed him, Cheng would have retired earlier. He could not understand why they treated him in such way. What could they achieve from creating difficulties for him? Could all these things be evidence to show he was not a real scientist?

Afterwards, Cheng was once again questioned, this time on how to kill chickens. How senseless it was! In their opinion, chickens and all other birds come from common ancestry. If Cheng did not know how to kill chickens, how could he call himself a real ornithologist? How ridiculous it was.

One day, however, higher officials unexpectedly arranged for him to help translate Darwin's famous *The Theory of Evolution*. It was learned afterwards that the book had been published for leaders of the Central Committee of the Party to read. Cheng thought that, surely there were other ways than asking

114

specialists to translate the book?

During the Cultural Revolution foreign guests often came to visit the Institute of Zoology. Their interpreter knew very little about ornithology. What should they do? They did not want to be embarrassed in front of foreigners. So Cheng was asked to work as an interpreter. After this officials asked him to teach young researchers English, which he was delighted to do. He gave lectures three hours a day, twice a week. After one class had finished, he was asked to run another. When the courses had finished, Cheng realised how much he had enjoyed being able to help others with his specialist knowledge.

GERMANY AND THE
SOVIET UNION

In 1955, East Germany sent a research team to China. They co-operated with scientists from the Chinese Academy of Sciences to research birds and mammals in north-eastern China. One of the German biologists was from the Berlin Museum.

In May 1957, the Chinese Academy of Sciences sent Cheng Tso-hsin on a return visit to East Germany to exchange information about birds. Cheng thought that it was a good opportunity for him to learn from foreign colleagues. He was invited to attend the East Europe Conference of Nature Conservation soon after he arrived in Berlin. Both the Chinese Forest Ministry and Chinese Academy of Sciences now asked him to attend it on their behalves. It was the first time that a Chinese scientist had attended an international conference on nature conservation and in addition to Cheng there were about 30 delegates from the Soviet Union, Bulgaria, Czechoslovakia, Yugoslavia, Finland, Poland, Hungary and East Germany. Representatives from the eastern European countries presented some good papers on the state of nature conservation. Cheng presented a paper entitled The Zoogeographical Regions and Endemic and Rare Species of Birds in China.

Although the conference only lasted a few days the scientists benefitted greatly from it, exchanging important ideas and information about conservation measures in each other's countries. China is a vast country with enormous variations in nature and rich in natural resources, the species of animals and plants differing within the areas. However not only were there no local organizations for nature conservation, but also no overall programme for conserving Chinese wildlife. After his return to China Cheng wrote a paper to the authorities, both reporting on the conference and also proposing ways to heighten the awareness of nature conservation in China.

Cheng stayed in Berlin from late May to the end of July. He spent most of his time undertaking research in the zoological museum, where he often met Prof Stresemann, the famous international ornithologist, and they exchanged some ideas on bird research. At that time Stresemann was very busy compiling *The Distribution Atlas of Breeding Birds in Europe* in co-

117

operation with Dr Portenko, an ornithologist from the Soviet Union. An American ornithologist, Dr Vaurie, had discussed with Dr Portenko the verification of some new sub-species of birds and both of them had insisted on their own viewpoints. Stresemann and Cheng mediated in the dispute. Prof Stresemann highly praised this discussion and said that it should be called a pan-Pacific academic conference.

During his stay Cheng visited the National Building (already in ruins), and went to the Bird Study Station at Seebach in the south. He also visited the famous Berlin Zoo. Berlin Zoo, founded in 1841, covers about 30 hectares and 2400 species of animals with more than 3000 birds of 900 species kept there. One side of the animal house was made from glass fibre reinforced plastic, which was much better than the steel wire because visitors could see the animals clearly through the glass and take photographs easily as well. Thus the behaviour of gorillas, lions, tigers and leopards could be observed without any disturbance from outside sound and also prevented visitors from provoking and feeding the animals.

The big, open cage for birds was about seven to eight metres high, with trees, grass, rockeries and brooks made to look like natural habitats. There were about 100 birds in this large aviary. Visitors could walk inside it by entering through a dark tunnel, which reduced disturbance. The behaviour of the birds was better in the walk-through aviary than in the small simple cages which housed the other birds.

On his way home Cheng dropped in to the Soviet Union for a week. In order to pay his respects to the remains of Lenin he went to Moscow first, visiting the Red Square and the Lenin Mausoleum. Then he flew to Leningrad (now St Petersberg) where he was given a warm welcome by Dr Ivanov, a famous ornithologist and vice-president of the Museum of Leningrad. There were about 140,000 specimens preserved in the Museum and a large number from China, most of which could not be seen in China, and which had been collected during the Tsarist period. It took Cheng a long time to examine them and to take notes. Because time was too limited he could not examine the Chinese bird specimens in detail, but nevertheless his visit was fruitful. During his stay the Soviet Government generously provided some financial support for his living expenses. Cheng saved some money, and bought professional books and field equipment with what he had left over. On returning to China he donated all of them to the Institute of Zoology, Chinese Academy of Science.

In 1958 Cheng again visited the Soviet Union. As early as the summer of 1957 the Soviet Union had sent a research team to China to investigate the birds in Yunnan province. Dr Ivanov was one of ten researchers in the team. The Chinese Academy of Sciences had selected a group of scientists to accompany their Soviet colleagues, of which Cheng was the second in command. On arrival in Yunnan, they undertook fieldwork every day. During daylight they surveyed and collected specimens while in the evening they organised and recorded their findings. They co-operated very happily.

After three months the Soviet team returned home, but not before inviting Chinese scientists to visit the Soviet Union. In April 1958 Cheng was recommended by the Chinese Academy of Sciences to pay a three-month visit. At the time he was preparing to go to Yunnan to collect birds and his luggage had already been sent to Guiyang, the captial of Guizhou province. On receiving the invitation, the director of the institute, Mr Liu Jiao-fe, helped him telegraph

Guiyang to ask friends to send the luggage back, but while it was still on its way Cheng had to leave for Moscow.

At the Airport he was welcomed by his friends from the National Natural Conservation Committee and representatives of the department of biology, University of Moscow and put into a luxury hotel. Cheng visited the University of Moscow first. It was very much an international university and at that time many Chinese students studied there. A Chinese restaurant had been specially set up and Cheng was invited to have a sumptuous Chinese lunch there.

He was invited to lecture at the department of biology, with its chairman, Prof Dementiev presiding over the seminar. Prof Dementiev was a famous ornithologist and editor-in-chief of *The Avifauna of the Soviet Union.* Cheng gave a good lecture on his research work in China after which many students asked him questions about the numbers of birds found in China, the distribution of tits, and the results of eliminating sparrows.

While he was in Moscow, Cheng spent most of his time studying the specimens of Chinese birds in the Museum but he also managed to visit some nature

121

reserves and bird-ringing centres. There were many saiga (a species of antelope) raised in the Astrakhan Nature Reserve near the Caspian Sea in the south of the Soviet Union, rumoured to have been founded on Lenin's order after the October Revolution. The Oksskji Bird-ringing Centre was in the middle of the Soviet Union, a mountainous forested area called 'green island in the desert'. As there were no roads and railways nearby, the only way to the centre area was by helicopter. The centre was equipped with every type of instrument and with a huge plastic net for capturing and ringing birds.

In Leningrad, Dr Ivanov accompanied Cheng to visit the Institute of Zoology. The facilities here were very good, with optical and electronic devices in common use. The specimens were displayed in wooden cases or boxes and arranged on shelves by families. Some specimen rooms also used lead and steel cases. Cheng took the opportunity to study specimens of Chinese birds, checking and classifing materials and taking notes of the specimens he was interested in.

The director of the Institute, Prof Pavlovskji, invited Cheng and several Chinese overseas students to a banquet in a restaurant called the Family of Scientists. After the banquet, Cheng presented him with a picture of shrimps drawn by Qi Baishi, a world famous artist. Prof Pavlovskji was very delighted.

In Leningrad, Cheng also met Mrs Kozlov, an ornithologist of the old school. They talked, exchanged information, and Dr and Mrs Ivanov invited Cheng to their house for dinner. On his return to China, Cheng passed through Siberia. At the Institute of Zoology at Irkutusk, near Lake Baikal. Professor Ckalon welcomed Cheng. Next morning, the Institute hired a steamer. The Baikal Lake is the largest freshwater lake in the world. There are 27 small islands and two bays, more than 1,500 species of animals and 1000 species of plants which include 70,000 seals, 900,000 sables, more than 100 species of birds, bears, deer and cats and several nature reserves had been established.

CHINESE BIRDS AND ZOO-GEOGRAPHY

After the *Checklist of Chinese birds* was published in 1947, Cheng Tso-hsin realised that his investigation into the resources of Chinese birds would not be sufficiently thorough if he only relied on the collection of foreign material. What was needed was for him to develop an overall investigation of the birds in China, by both collecting more specimens and obtaining information on the breeding, ecology and distribution of each species. Such an arduous task could not be done by one person. It would require strong leadership, thorough organisation, and a great deal of co-operation. So a thorough investigation into the resources of Chinese birds began, organised and controlled by the Chinese Academy of Sciences. It was what Cheng proposed and what he wanted.

From the 1950s, Cheng Tso-hsin took part in or organised almost all the explorations into the bird resources every year. From 1953 to 1956 he went to the fruit-growing district of Changli, Hebei province. In 1953-1954, he investigated the insect-eating birds at Weishan Lake, Shandong province. In 1956-1957, he was in charge of a ten-strong team of young Chinese scientists who took part in the Sino-Soviet Union subtropical natural resource in Yunnan province. In 1957-1958, he led a team to Hunan province, and to Hainan island in 1960. In 1957-1960, he designed and took part in the bird investigation related to the 'Dislocating water from the south northward project' organised by the Chinese Academy of Sciences. After 1960 he was in charge of the animal research group in the Tibet - Qinghai Plateau expedition. From 1974-1976 he investigated waterfowl in north-eastern China and in the south of Yangtze river.

For several decades, Cheng and his colleagues surveyed around China: the Emei mountains, Songpan grassland, many hills and lakes around the Yellow River and Yangtze River basin, Dawei mountain in Yunnan, Wuzhi Mountain in Hainan, Zhalong region, Dailing and Changbai mountain in the north-east. The places where bird habitats are good are usually sparsely populated, with steep mountains and thick forests. The living conditions were usually sparten and in some places, even dangerous.

The fieldwork was very hard. He frequently 'ate in the wind and slept in the dew' and worked day and night. In the 1950s when they studied the breeding and lifestyles of insect-eating birds in the woodland of Changli, Hebei province, they worked round the clock, watching continuously at nest sites. Sometimes they would lie on the ground in the forest without moving, to observe birds before dawn.

Once, when he was 50, Cheng was undertaking exploration on Huangshan mountain when he fell down on a very steep road and had to crawl. As a result, his new trousers became 'a pair with many holes'. Shortly after his return, a meeting was due to be held in the capital of the province. Cheng attended with his 'special' trousers, and made something of an exhibition of himself.

In Sichuan province in an area where the mountains were very high and the paths difficult to climb, Cheng and his colleagues had to scramble over rocks and roots in order to collect specimens. It was very dangerous and one little mistake would result in a fall. Once they had to cross a stream, which as they understood later was directly connected with an uphill reservoir built for collecting logs. When the reservoir

126

became packed with wood, the loggers opened the sluice gate to let the wood float down with the current. When Cheng and his party approached the stream, the gates were just being opened. Someone cried, "don't hurry!" But the party heard it as "hurry up" because they did not understand the local accent. So they hurried up; just after two young fellows had stepped into the stream the logs came down and the person in front of the team was washed away. Cheng was just a few metres behind. The whole team was very sad about the accident. Fieldwork is hard and dangerous, far beyond what most people can imagine. But if evidence has to be collected to make progress in scientific research, the risk must be taken.

Another time, in Dawei Shan in Yunnan province, the path was so narrow that only a donkey could pass. Since they had been travelling day and night, the donkeys were tired, and one donkey loaded with boxes and packages of many fine specimens fell into a deep abyss. Cheng himself fell from the back of his horse and hurt his ribs causing many days of pain. This was the tour on which Cheng and his colleagues discovered a new subspecies of Laughing Thrush - the Daweishan subspecies.

After many years of hard work, they collected thousands of bird specimens, and gathered a great deal of first hand information about their ecology and distribution. There are now more than 60,000 - a huge number - of specimens in the Institute of Zoology, and it is the biggest museum of bird specimens in China. It is about more than 20 times the size of the collections in Beijing Zoological Institute and Jing-Shen Biological Institute before liberation.

Nowadays when Cheng recalls the fieldwork of the old days, he says with deep feeling: "So many people worked so hard to explore and collect all this first hand material. Although we have already taken strenuous efforts in making new discoveries, we should come to realise that the natural world is a treasure-house for scientific research. At the same time, we should all understand and appreciate the magnificent treasures of our homeland."

Each time he came back from the field, Cheng arranged the collected specimens, identified and recorded them. He printed the Latin names and worked over the synonyms. Sometimes he would take several days in examining one specimen. The less reference material there was the longer it took.

Over about ten years, Cheng came across thousands of specialist papers and books. During identification, it was neccessary to compare specimens and related materials. Many of them were kept in museums and research institutes abroad so it is was necessary to travel. In 1945, Cheng took the opportunity when he was a visiting professor to the USA, to check up many types of specimens of Chinese species in the New York Museum of Natural History and accumulated much useful material. After liberation, he also visited the Institute of Zoology in Leningrad in the Soviet Union, the Berlin Museum in Germany, the Paris Museum in France and the British Museum in England. After China and the USA established diplomatic relations, he visited the USA twice again. He went to the National Museum of USA, New York Museum of Natural History and the museums at Harvard and Michigan Universities to do research.

It is the new China that gave Cheng the opportunity to investigate the specimens of Chinese birds scattered abroad, especially those of new species. As a result, the number of reference cards becomes larger and larger and the knowledge of China's birds and the details of each species became clearer and clearer.

For countless hot summers and cold winters, Cheng was too busy to have a holiday. Even on the traditional China Spring Festival holiday, Cheng still worked in his office. Finally he was able to produce a monumental work *Distributional List of Chinese Birds* (published in two volumes) in 1955 and 1958. In these Cheng listed both the scientific names and the synonyms and showed the distribution of each bird species and sub-species clearly. It was both clear and thorough, and was very well received in academic circles. The book soon sold out but scientists both in China and overseas wrote continuously asking for the book. The Science Press then invited Cheng to revise the work and the second edition was published in 1978.

* * * * * *

Based on the data he had collected on the status and distribution of China's birds, Cheng Tso-hsin found that the zoogeographical regions delineated by foreign biologists did not really reflect the situation accurately. China has two of the six geographic realms on earth, the Palearctic and the Oriental. It is very rare that sizable portions of the two realms occur in one country, which explains the richness of China's biodiversity.

On the boundary of these two realms A. Wallace, a British biologist and the founder of Zoogeography, presented in 1876 his view that the line of demarcation should be in the Nanling mountains. This had been accepted by biologists over the years.

But having worked on the birds and mammals for many years Cheng and his colleagues thought this boundary did not coincide with the real distribution of Chinese land vertebrates. Based on their long-term investigations and studies, they thought it should be shifted northward to Qingling mountains. In 1959, Cheng and his colleague, Zhang Rong-zu, complied *The Dividing of Zoological Regions in China* in which they had analysed the distribution of the endemic species, dominant species and the main economic species of birds and mammals, and agreed scientifically why Qingling mountains should be the border between the Palearctic and the Oriental realms. Their evidence covered not only the faunal diversities

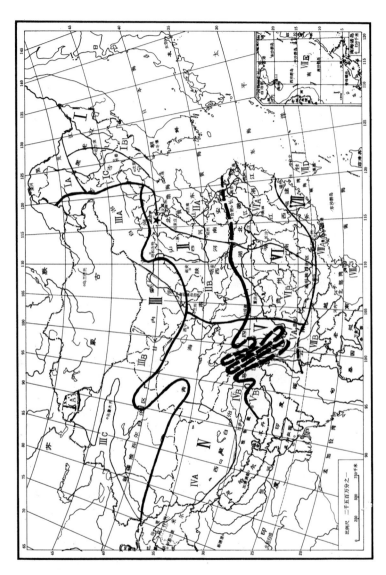

Avifaunal regionalization of China

Order of Regions	Realms	Sub-realms	I-order: Regions	II-order : Subregions	Numbering of Regions
NAMES of DIVISIONS	Palaearctic Realm (一)	(A) East-Asian Realm	I North-east Region	IA Da-Xingan Mt. Subregion I(A) Altai Mt. Subregion	1
				IB Changbei Mt. Subregion	2
				IC Song-Liao Plain Subregion	3
			II North-China Region	IIA Huang-Huai Plain Subregion	4
				IIB Loess Plateau Subregion	5
		(B) Eremian Subrealm	III Mongo-Xinjiang Region	IIIA East Meadow Subregion	6
				IIIB West Desert Subregion	7
				IIIC Tianshan Hilly Subregion	8
	Oriental Realm (二)	(C) Central Asian Subrealm	IV Qinghai-Xizang Region	IVA Qiantang Plateau Subregion	9
				IVB Qinghai-Zangnan Subregion	10
		(D) Sino-Indian Subrealm	V Southwest Region	VA Southwest Mountainous Subregion	11
				VB Southeast Himalayan Slope Subregion	12
			VI Mid-China Region	VIA Eastern Hillock-Plain Subregion	13
				VIB Western Mountainous Plateau Subregion	14
			VII South China Region	VIIA Min-Quang Coastal Subregion	15
				VIIB Southern Yunnan Hilly Subregion	16
				VIIC Hainan Subregion	17
				VIID Taiwan Subregion	18
				VIIE South-sea Islands Subregion	19

133

of birds and mammals, but also ranges of soils, vegetation and climates. It was adopted by most scientists.

Still not content, Cheng and Zhang Rong-zu undertook further dividing of the geographical regions of China based on their own research. They divided the two realms into four sub-realms, seven regions and 19 sub-regions (see Table on page 133). This scheme of geographical division had much scientific significance instantaneously.

Cheng divided the Palearctic realm of China into three sub-realms, East Asia, Central Asia and Eremian. The last one was named for the first time and it combines the deserts in northern China with the dry areas of mid-Asia and those of Arab countries, and the Sahara desert in northern Africa - all linked together to form an unique landscape zone across the northern hemisphere in the old world. Because of all the contributions he made in the field of zoo-geography with international significance, Cheng was recognised as a pioneer of Chinese zoogeography. The zoogeographical divisions of China which he and Zhang Rong-zu made have now been adopted universally by scientists.

We do not know if Cheng's achivements in zoogeography were a result of his hard study of geography using the map on the wall in his early years. But there is no doubt that he has a very clear memory of the map of China. In his *Chinese Avifauna*, published in 1987, he presents the distribution ranges of all the 1186 species of birds known at that time so that the readers can easily identify how many birds there are in a certain area and in which realm and which region a certain species of birds belongs to. It is a very important reference book, not only for professional ornithologists but also for birdwatchers in general.

* * * * * *

In 1957, Cheng Tso-hsin's *Distributional List of Chinese Birds, Vol.2 Passeriformes* was published by the Science Press and received high praise from academic circles. But the edition was so limited that it was not available in the bookstores quickly although very much in demand. Many who could not buy it wrote to the publishers who then invited him to update it for a second edition.

135

This took several years. When finished, the manuscript was nearly one metre high and represented the fruits of expeditions and study over many years. He had worked his heart out to make it the first comprehensive and systematic analysis of Chinese birds so far known by their scientific names, gathering and reorganizing new data concerning their classification, rectifying the differentiation of sub-species, evolutionary tendencies, ecology, distribution and migration. The manuscript was sent to the Science Press to be printed.

But then a political hurricane descended. The Cultural Revolution began with the cry "the more knowledge you have, the more reactionary you are considered to be". Scientific research stopped. Every day was filled with writing endless dazibao and attending critical meetings. The library and the specimen rooms were closed. Because of lack of management, some references and specimens were spoiled or lost. Academic magazines stopped publishing. Research institutes and publishing houses almost disintegrated. Science was like a tree in winter, dwindling and withering.

During the days when the Gang of Four were

running wild, Cheng was isolated to 'introspection'. The Gang of Four said that birds were pets of the capitalist. If a socialist country studied them, it would be revisionism and the country would be ruined. Therefore, Cheng must be downgraded. The typesetting of his revised manscript of *Distributional List of Chinese Birds* was ordered to be stopped in the publishing house and to be returned to him for criticism. Xie Zhong-ping, an editor of the publishing house who was very responsible, understood the value of the manuscript and kept it carefully. But by the end of 1969 even he couldn't keep out of trouble. Just before he was transferred to Cadre school for reform, he mailed the manuscript, double registered, to the Institute of Zoology, Chinese Academy of Sciences, where Cheng worked.

At that time, the Institute had been renamed Revolutionary Rebellion Group and it was known as a Commune. He was imprisoned in a 'cowshed', sweeping courtyards and cleaning lavatories every day. His precious manuscript was received by someone in power and was then thrown away as rubbish somewhere unknown. Cheng did not mind being isolated but what really worried him was the fate of his manuscript. To his enquiries came the answer "Just wait! Someone will tell you when it is sent back." Cheng could say nothing. He looked back on his life and was content, and saw more clearly through the Gang of Four's ferocious nature. Although confined to a small room, what constantly worried him was his research work and collections. His life had been linked closely to those beautiful mountains, green forests and lovely birds. He understood deeply nature and birds, and it was as if nature and birds also had a feeling for him. When he was immersed in this vision he recalled a poem which said, "Wild geese lead an anxious heart to go far away, mountains draw the pleasant moon to come closer" and it seemed that all beautiful birds were flying up to him.

In 1974 Premier Zhou En-lai pointed out that the study of the basic theories could not be ignored and then in 1975, Deng Xiao-ping took charge of the routine national matters again. These changes brought him hope, like a breath of fresh air. The turbulent times had made the hair on Cheng's temples turn grey. Ten years had gone by, during which time there had been no sign of his manuscript.

138

After the Gang of Four had been crushed, he wrote to the editor to ask about his manuscript, but the answer shook him. Xie Zhong-ping told him that it had been mailed back to him several years before. Where was it? He made inquiries, but nobody admitted to having received it or having seen it. He searched in the archives and administrative departments but no one knew about it. He was very sad. "For this book, I spent tens of years of my life and went to so many places, collected so many specimens and so much data, and the State spent so much money, so much manpower and so much in material resources! All of these are wasted!" Then one day after some time, someone hurried to his home and told him that a manuscript had been found in the storeroom.

Cheng was so excited that he could not remember running to the storeroom beside the library. He was nearly 70 years old, but he rushed to the gloomy little room like a young man. He saw paper and old publications scattered everywhere. It was lucky it had not all been thrown out as waste paper. He saw his manuscript among them. It was as if a 'child' who has been lost for many years now appeared in front of him again. He bowed his head, the tears dropping down on the manuscript beside his feet. The pages were not in order, but kind-hearted colleagues helped him collect them one by one. Nevertheless quite a few diagrams and maps could not be found.

But Cheng comforted his colleagues, "It is very fortunate to find most of the manuscript; the lost part does not matter much and can be replaced without too much difficulty."

The historic third session of the 11th Chinese Communist Party Congress was held at the end of 1978. An entire new epoch appeared after the Chinese Communist Party brought order out of chaos. The second edition of Cheng Tso-hsin's book *Distributional List of Chinese Birds* was also published in that year. When Cheng visited America in 1981, his *Alma Mater*, the University of Michigan awarded him an honour for publishing the book.

* * * * * *

In the book *Mottos of Modern Chinese Scientists*, there is one from Cheng Tso-hsin which says, "To love nature, it is most important that you learn from

140

the live book of nature". The pinnacle of science is glittering and everyone wants to reach it, but the road to the top is very hard to achieve, like climbing a path full of stones and prickly shrubs. For several decades Cheng never stopped climbing to the summit of ornithology up such a difficult path.

For many years, from spring to autumn, he was normally out in the mountain forests with birds. He only 'hibernated' in his house during the snowy winter after most birds had migrated. In the 1950s the Chinese Academy of Sciences organized some explorations on biological resources and Cheng was an active participant. For example, in the late 1950s the Academy formed a multi-disciplined survey team to work on the national project of 'dislocating water from the south to the north'. The research team was composed of more than 100 scientists from many fields including zoology, botany, mineralogy and meteorology. Cheng led the zoological research of ten zoologists to survey wildlife in the vast areas from the Ermei mountain to Aba grassland in Sichuan province. The road was very hard to walk as it was muddy with soft grass and sharp stones underneath.It was the same road that the Red Army crossed during

141

the famous Long March in the 1930s and it was hard to undertake research in that area.

There were two base camps of the survey team, one in Huidong and another in Leibo. One day Marshal Nie Rong-zhen and Zhu Ke-zhen, one of the vice presidents of the Academy, came to see the scientists. Marshal Nie was a famous commander of the Chinese Army in the war and in charge of science and technology after the founding of the People's Republic of China. Marshal Nie had lunch with the scientists, enquired about the progress of the surveys and asked about their health with deep concern. He was a nice man, easy going and without pretence. He encouraged the scientists to insist on surveys in order to obtain more first-hand material.

At that time, Cheng was about 50 years old. He worked as hard as the young scientists, climbing mountains and crossing rivers. They went from Liangshan, Huidong, Leibo to Miyi, Yanyuan, Muli of Xichang areas and finally into Lushui, Lijiang, Deqin of north western Yunnan. They did not return to Beijing until August 1960, when they had finished the survey.

In the late period of the Cultural Revolution, when

he had just got back the right to work, he asked eagerly if he could conduct an investigation into the waterfowl in the Yangtze River. He was over 70 years old. This was agreed and he and his colleague were given permits to carry out survey work in the area.

In the early spring it was cold out in the country. Cheng took a sampan (a small boat) on the Dongting lake. He wore a heavy coat and searched the lake carefully to count waterfowl. The Dongting lake is one of the large lakes in the south and it is very beautiful. A few hours after he had started a small fishing boat approached the sampan. A little boy rowed, while a middle-aged man stood. When it came close enough the man shouted, "I am Yu Jia-wang. A fishery commune sent me to extend a welcome to Prof Cheng, the guest from Beijing..."

Yu Jia-wang was the person to whom he had been given an introduction. He and his colleague changed to the fishing boat and thanked the owner of the sampan for his help. Yu Jia-wang talked, laughed, and was very excited at meeting Prof Cheng. He introduced his son, and he introduced him to the waterfowl on the lake as well. Yu Jia-wang was an experienced fisherman. When they arrived at his house, Yu Jia-wang began to prepare dinner. He cooked fresh fish and large lobsters and, as he cooked the meal, he ordered his son to go to the lake for more food.

The little boy answered his father happily and disappeared. A few minutes later, two gun shots could be heard, and the boy came back with two duck. After the dinner, Yu Jia-wang led them to the lake. It was dusk. He fired a shot and immediately a large flock of birds took off. A few minutes later, the wild ducks and geese landed and hid in the grass again. It was wonderful habitat for waterfowl. Today the Dongting marshland is an important nature reserve for waterfowl and it is also listed as one of the important wetlands in the International Wetland Convention.

Cheng had been to many remote areas in China - the forests of Daweishan of Yunnan, Wuzhishan of Hainan, Hulun lake of Inner Mongolia, Zhalong, Dailing and Changbai mountains of the north eastern part of China. He went to these areas not to enjoy the beautiful scenery but to collect specimens and undertake research. No matter how tired he was from a long journey or the hardship of sleeping in the forest or the danger of climbing cliffs, he kept at his

Exploring in the Wu-Lu-Shan district, Inner Mongolia (September 1971).

scientific work. It was Cheng's work as well as his pleasure to stay in the grass on the bank of the lake and watch the birds day and night, or hide in the forest to study the behaviour of birds.

In 1975 Cheng reached the Heavenly Lake in the Changbai mountains. The Heavenly Lake is 2,600 meters above the sea level, formed after a volcanic eruption many years ago. Originally it was a big cave

145

caused by the eruption which then filled with clean water. The lake looks like a mirror inlaid in the blue sky, white clouds and the green mountains. Because of the high altitude and low air pressure, no fish live in the lake.

Cheng's colleagues tried to persuade him not get to the Heavenly Lake as he had a heart problem and high blood pressure. But he insisted: "I have already come this far; I cannot give up halfway. I must reach the top." Then he began to walk up. Although he could not go up very quickly he did not need support from his friends and that he finally reached the Heavenly Lake gave him great pleasure. He had learned a lot from the trip to Changbai mountains. He found that the vertical variations of the landscape were very significant, and the border of the four zones of vegetation was very clear. At the bottom, the zone consisted of broadleaf trees and the Korean pines. The second zone is the dark coniferous forest, dominated mainly by firs. The third is the deciduous forest made up of oak and birch. At the top is the tundra where there are no trees. The unique landscape variations cannot be seen so clearly in other areas. The richness of plant diversity results in an abundance of wildlife resources. According to their survey, there are 277 species of birds in Changbai mountains. Among them, many species are nationally protected.

At that time, knowing Cheng had high blood pressure and heart-disease, his wife and children were very worried about him. They had not received letters but finally Cheng returned to Beijing after a long and arduous journey.

In the same year he also went to Zhalong, located in Qiqihar city of Heilongjiang province to study birds. As a result of their studies, Cheng and his colleagues proposed to the government of Qiqihar city and the forest department of Heilongjiang province the establishment of a nature reserve in Zhalong to protect the rare red-crowned crane. After he returned to Beijing, he made the same proposal to the forest department of China. A year later, the first nature reserve for the protection of birds in China, Zhalong National Nature Reserve, was established and the red-crowned crane has been protected by law in China ever since. Later on, many other nature reserves were set up, including the Bird Island of Qinghai Lake (for bar-headed geese and other waterfowl), Pangquangou Nature Reserve and Luyashan Nature Reserve in

Shanxi province, Xiao Wutaishan Nature Reserve in Heibei province (for brown eared-pheasants) and so on.

From 1956-1980, Cheng was in charge of the biological group of the Qinghai-Tibet Plateau multi-disciplied survey team. He published two books: *Birds of Xizang (Tibet)*, and *On the land-vertebrate fauna of Qinghai-Tibetan Plateau with consideration concerning its history of transforamtion*, both publications won high appraisals in China.

OVERSEAS VISITS

The World Pheasant Association was founded in 1975 by enthusiasts who kept and bred endangered species of pheasants in captivity for the purpose of saving them from extinction. At that time more than a third of the 49 species of pheasants were threatened. The WPA promoted the preservation of pheasants in its early years and then became the eminent international conservation organisation for all the galliformes, which include pheasants, grouse, partridges, quails and francolins, megapodes and cracids.

In order to promote international academic exchange the WPA holds an international symposium every three or four years. The aims of the Association are to support, advance and develop the conservation of all species of galliformes. It encourages people in both native and non-native countries to use suitable ways to keep pheasants and to establish a reference system or database of galliformes to serve its members and other organisations in ecological research, nature reserve management, wildlife conservation and aviculture. The WPA tries to

149

develop field research techniques and improve captive breeding levels. It publishes scientific papers and professional books on galliformes, carries out education programmes and helps set up breeding centres for endangered species among other things.

In 1978 the WPA invited Cheng Tso-hsin to visit the UK in December and attend the Woodland Grouse Symposium in Inverness, Scotland, which they were sponsoring. After obtaining permission from the authorities, 73-year-old Cheng and his postgraduate student, Lu Tai-chun, went to Britain. It was his first visit to a foreign country after the Cultural Revolution.

They arrived in London on 21 November 1978. The former chairman of the World Pheasant Association, Mr Kit Savage, and the director of the Wildfowl Trust, Mr Matthews met them at the Airport. In the evening a reception was held by leaders and members of the WPA including Kit Savage, Timothy and Diana Lovel, Keith and Jean Howman and Iain and Didy Grahame. The party was lively and memorable, bursting with humour and good cheer both there and throughout the ensuing dinner. They were full of zest, wit and humour. It

Professor Cheng at the Woodland Grouse Symposium.

remains a very happy memory for Cheng's.

After the party, Keith Howman, a founder WPA council member at that time, then later chairman and now its director general, invited Cheng to stay in his house, a beautiful place beside the river Thames, both peaceful and secluded. The house was permeated with a scholar's atmosphere. Keith and his lovely wife, Jean, were very kind and prepared a large and comfortable room for Cheng and his student. After such a long journey he was so tired that he fell asleep

151

very quickly. The next morning, after breakfast, the hosts took Cheng on a tour of their grounds, which were considerable and which housed probably the largest pheasant collection in the world. Among notable species were grey peacock-pheasant, Palawan peacock-pheasant, bronze-tailed peacock-pheasant, green peafowl and the great argus which is native to Malaysia. Peacock-pheasants are rare ornamental birds. There are many dots and speckles in the male's plumage. The head has a hair-like crest and a pair of eye-like speckles appear on the tail. It is similar to the peafowl but much smaller, so it is called the peacock-pheasant. The female peacock-pheasant is slightly smaller than the cock whose plumage is darker than that of the female.

In the centre of the grounds was a lovely lake which held many waterfowl. Cheng recognised several species such as Canada geese, mute swans, mallard and moorhens. To the south of the lake, there were cages with francolin, partridges and quail. Among them were common hill-partridge which occur in China, Madagascar partridge from the island of that name, grey francolin from India and California quail from north America.

Many rare pheasant species can be found here. Beside the cheer pheasant from Pakistan, red junglefowl from India, crested fireback from southeast Asia, Siamese fireback from Thailand, bar-faced curassow from south America, there were pheasant species from China such as brown eared, white eared, golden, Lady Amherst's, Reeves's and silver pheasants. China is rich in pheasants; half of the pheasant species of the world are found there.

In the grounds Cheng also saw a pair of Blyth's tragopan, usually found in south-eastern Tibet, northwestern Yunnan in China and the surrounding areas of Burma and India. In the wild, Blyth's tragopan live in the dense forest at an altitude of 1800 to 4000 meters above sea level. The wild population is very scarce. In the past only one male specimen was collected by Chinese researchers in Gaoligong Shan in Yunnan province, so Cheng was very excited to see the live birds in the Howman collection.

The second place Cheng visited was the British Natural History Museum at Tring, about 50 km from London, where he spent some time examining specimens of Chinese birds. The Museum is regarded as very valuable by the British government and is protected by guards day and night. More than 1,500,000 bird specimens collected from all over the world are stored here (including 10,000 from China). One of the oldest of these is a bird collected in Yunnan in 1820. There are also 800 specimens of rare species and sub-species, 5000 nests and 100,000 eggs including 655 nests and 2944 eggs from China. Apart from these, there are more than 8000 bird skeletons and the 1200 formaldehyde-preserved specimens in the Museum as well.

Staff at the Museum work in three groups, avian taxonomy, avian skeleton study and avian nest and egg study. As the study of avifauna had been completed in Britain a long time ago, the researchers in the Museum had started to compile data of the avifauna of the world. They were working on projects such as *The Crows of the World*, *The Pigeons and Doves of the World*, *The Atlas of Breeding Birds in Africa*, and were classifying birds collected from the developing countries in order to find new species and sub-species in the lesser known areas.

The Museum has a field research station to study behaviour, activity, breeding ecology, population dynamics of wild birds and to obtain the first-hand information from the natural world. The staff use modern techniques such as audio equipment and sonographs to study bird songs, advanced remote sensing, radiotelemetry and computers to study bird migrations, and X-ray machines combined with micro-cameras to study bird skeletons. Another advantage of the Museum is that all the specimen cabinets and drawers are made of special plastic, which is not only light and easy to move but also prevents them from being eaten by worms. Thus plastic equipment for storing specimens was perhaps only found in the British Museum at that time.

The Museum not only owns a large number of specimens but keeps a great many books and reference materials as well. The library holds more than 200,000 professional books and about 400 ornithological journals from all over the world in many languages including English, Chinese, French, Japanese, Russian and Korean. There is also a special room which holds out-of-print books and other rare publications. The Museum has become one of the centres of international bird study and every year thousands of bird researchers from many countries come here to work.

155

At four o'clock in the afternoon every working day there is a tea break in the Museum. Staff gather in the common room and talk among themselves while drinking tea or coffee. When he studied in the Museum, Cheng joined in on several discussions. This kind of discussion after hard work is not only a rest but also a good chance for scientists to meet each other and exchange ideas.

After the research work at the Natural History Museum, Cheng and his student visited the Wildfowl Trust. Prof Matthews, the director, took them in his car to show them waterfowl, swans, the bird-ringing station, the marshland used to attract wild waterfowl and the research institute. As there was so much to be seen and so much to take in, they were very tired and especially Prof Matthews who had to drive and to explain everything. Cheng will never forget Prof Matthews's great kindness. He really enjoyed the visit to the Wildfowl Trust, where he saw and learned a lot.

In the swan area, there was a small hut equipped with glass windows through which Cheng saw a big flock of some 1000 swans, part of which was flying, and part of which remained on the lake. What a beautiful sight it was, the water of the lake clean and green, with the white swans swimming on it. There were so many wonderful things that he simply could not take them all in, but it all left Cheng feeling happy.

The swans are fed by staff at a regular time every evening. Because there are flood-lights it seems like daytime when the swans are fed at night. Many swans from the surrounding areas also come to seek food and all of them compete for it being unafraid of vistors. It was really a wonderful experience for Cheng; it was beyond his expectations to see such a marvellous place in the countryside of Britain.

On 1 December, Cheng went to the headquarters of the Wildfowl Trust at Slimbridge, which is near the west coast of Britain. The Trust, founded by the late Sir Peter Scott in 1946, is the earliest and also the largest waterfowl reserve in Britain. Sir Peter was a famous bird-lover, painter and writer. When he was young, he had enjoyed wildfowling through which, after a long period of hunting, he became very knowledgeable. Subsequently he stopped hunting and channelled all his energies and considerable funds into conservation, finally establishing eight waterfowl centres and viewing places in Britain.

The headquarters of the Wildfowl Trust was divided into two parts. In the front it had a well-designed bird garden while in the back was a large lake for waterfowl. Walk into the Trust and you will find a cheerful world where both men and birds are friendly. There were about 2500 birds of 180 species raised there in 1978. It has become one of the largest collections and the best research institution for waterfowl in the world. The Mandarin duck of China and white-headed duck of Hungary are also kept there.

Across the lake is a nature reserve which is nine times as big as the bird garden. The most important feature in the reserve is that the birds live free while

Professor Cheng and Sir Peter Scott at Slimbridge, England (1978).

the visitors are not as free as the birds. Visitors go down a small path to the observation shed to watch the birds. Inside the shed are high-quality telescopes so that they can see birds in the distance very clearly. Handicapped visitors can go to the shed by wheelchairs and children have special chairs which are adjustable for height. In front of the shed is a large area of freshwater, marsh and grassland. In winter, huge numbers of duck, geese and swans arrive to overwinter. It is a magnificent sight. Cheng and his student stayed in the Wildfowl Trust for a couple of days. Then they went to Inverness to attend the Grouse Symposium.

The Conference took place in a luxury hotel and the hosts had left the best room for their Chinese guests. On 4 December, the conference opened with about 70-80 delegates attending from Britain, France, the United States, Soviet Union, Germany and China. Cheng presented two papers, *Taxonomic and ecological notes of Capercaillies and Black Grouse in China* and *A sketch of the avian fauna of China with special reference to galliforme species*. He was warmly applauded and his two papers were selected for publication in the proceedings of the Conference.

He was also interviewed on radio and elected a vice president of the WPA. He held this position three times before becoming president of the Association in 1986 when the Third International Pheasant Symposium took place in Thailand. It was the first time in the history of the WPA that its president was from China; indeed to this day he is the only Chinese person to be president of an international conservation organisation.

After the conference Didy Graham arranged for them to visit the Museum of Oxford University, the oldest natural history museum in the world and

Professor Cheng giving a plenary address at the 4th Interntional Pheasant Symposium held in October 1989 in Beijing.

Prof and Mrs Cheng holding photos of the brown eared-pheasant and the golden pheasant respectively, with Keith Howman standing behind (Beijing Symposium, 1989).

established in 1683 by Mr A Ashmolean. He had studied natural philosophy, mathematics and astronomy as a young man, had joined the government, met and married a rich widow enabling him to spend more time on his research and writing books. He helped found the Royal Society, becoming a member in 1663. In 1675, he received a Doctor Degree of Medical Science in Oxford University. In 1692, just before he died, he donated all his manuscripts and 1758 copies of books to the Museum which he had suggested and which had been

161

completed in 1683. Today, the Museum is the centre of scientific activity at Oxford University. On his visit to the University, Cheng gave a lecture to the students and some professors from the biology department in which he introduced the avifauna of China and the studies of Chinese birds. His paper was published in *Ibis*, a journal of The British Ornithological Union, which invited Cheng to become an overseas member.

Cheng was very impressed with the good behaviour of the citizens of London in that they did not disturb wildlife, or kill the birds or take eggs from their nests. There were thousands of wild pigeons in London which were very friendly to visitors and always looked for food. In some squares there are thousands of pigeons. Once they discover food in your hand, they will congregate around you, try to perch on your arms or peck your trousers in order to get it. Even the flocks of house sparrows imitate the pigeon and join the queue for food. Some audacious pigeons even go into the restaurants and the kitchens. It would be very easy to catch them if you wanted to but London citizens don't.

In the two months he stayed in the UK, Cheng received generous hospitality from many organizations and friends. His visit was very successful and fruitful. Not only had he introduced the achievements of Chinese ornithologists to foreign colleagues but he had also obtained many good ideas for research in China. Furthermore, he had rebuilt the bridge between Chinese and foreign researchers after the Cultural Revolution. On 20 December 1978, the Chinese Embassy in Britain held a return banquet to thank all the people who had provided Cheng with hospitality. The chairman of the World Pheasant Association, the director of the Wildfowl Trust, the chief of London Zoo and leaders from other organisations attended. Mr Hu Ding-yi, the Councillor of the Chinese Embassy, helped to organise it with many fresh vegetables and cooking materials flown specially from China, A superb Chinese meal was served which was much enjoyed by all who attended.

For his stay in Britain, the Chinese Academy of Sciences had provided Cheng with generous living expenses. However he and his student had lived frugally and been so generously hosted that they saved a lot of money. After his return to China, they handed it all back to the Academy; they felt that the money belonged to the country and it should be put to use where it was badly needed on more research on China's wildlife.

* * * * * *

In January 1980 the International Conference on Waterfowl and Cranes was held in Zhahuang, Hukkaido, Japan. It was sponsored by Japan and Britain, and China was invited by Japan. The Chinese Academy of Sciences asked Cheng Tso-hsin to lead a delegation to take part. When he arrived in Tokyo, Cheng was accorded lavish hospitality by the Yamashina Institute for Ornithology, the Wild Bird Association, the state-maintained Science Museum and other related organizations.

The Conference took place from January 15 to 24 in a hotel in Zhahuang and hundreds of people participated. Cheng, Ma Yiqing, Zhou Fuzhang and some others gave lectures and Cheng was interviewed almost every night. The interviews were published or broadcast the next day. When the delegation left, reporters presented Cheng with two autographed books containing newspaper cuttings of his talks and photographs of him speaking. He has kept them to this day.

164

While there, they also visited the Dahui Routine Bureau and the Dajing Park of wild birds. They also exchanged ideas with the members of the Japanese Wild Bird Association. One evening a symposium on the crested ibis was held. The bird's scientific name is *Nipponia nippon*, which in Latin means Japan, so many participants thought that the ibis was the symbol of Japan. During the symposium, Japanese scholars pointed out that there were only a few ibises left in Japan, living mainly around Zudu in Xin county where they were on the edge of extinction. The scholars wanted to find the best way to preserve them.

Experts from different countries stated their views and made suggestions. Cheng mentioned that four ibises had been caught in Qinling Range, China, in the early 1960s. This aroused much enthusiasm and cheerfulness at the symposium. Nevertheless China was still searching for ibis so Cheng expressed a wish to cooperate with his Japanese colleagues. So began a joint venture to protect and research wild birds without the limitations of national borders. Later in 1981 ibises were again found in China, breeding in small colonies. In Japan, the ibises were too old to breed, so they exchanged live birds with our country to keep the species alive.

165

Observing birds in the field (February 1980).

166

During the conference a visit to Baihiao Tai (Hundred Birds Platform) was organised. In front of it is not blue sea but a white 'sea' of countless swans, which was really magnificent. Later they visited the habitats of cranes, and saw many cranes 'dancing' in the air.

After the conference they were invited to visit Tokyo where, to everyone's surprise, there were thousands of wild birds living and breeding. At the Ren Pool in ShangYe Zoo, in 1962, 19 cormorants were imported from Qianye county and later thousands of cormorants were attracted to live there. There were 13 kinds of wild ducks which came to Ren Pool every October to overwinter. There were more than 6000. Now more and more waterfowl are attracted there, which makes the park even more beautiful. The state-maintained Science Museum in Tokyo also impressed them deeply, with the breadth of its collections, abundant funds and advanced equipment. The Science Museum featured exhibits about the adaptation and evolution of organisms, plants and animals in Japan and about the sun and the universe.

In November 1980, there were negotiations between China and Japan about the protection of migratory birds. The Chinese delegation was formed by the Ministry of Forestry, with Dong Zhiyong, the deputy Minister, as chairman. Cheng Tso-hsin and Tang Yangkuang were elected from the Academy of Sciences to be delegates. During the negotiations, the atmosphere was always mild and cordial. After the meeting a Japanese expert who had taken part wrote to Cheng and said that he had taken part in similar international negotiations but that this one was the most cordial and friendly, which pleased both sides greatly. Agreement was reached. The late Dr Yamashina, director of the Yamashina Institute for Ornithology gave a grand banquet to entertain the Chinese delegation and they also exchanged gifts.

The Agreement on the protection of migratory birds and their habitats between the People's Republic of China and Japan was offically signed on 3 March 1981. It included six clauses. There were 227 species of migratory birds listed in the agreement, comprising 45 per cent of the birds in Japan, 20 per cent of the birds in China. It was the first time China had signed an agreement concerning birds with another country.

Its significance is that both sides should support the protection of migratory birds, set up nature reserves for them and strengthen research so that endangered and rare species can be preserved. Both sides may use the resource of the dominant species legally to improve people's living standards.

Most birds are beneficial and useful to humans directly or indirectly. Moreover people often regard birds as a sign of peace. Not only did the agreement enhance the protection of birds, but it also consolidated and expanded the friendship between the Japanese and Chinese people.

* * * * * *

In April 1980, having been invited by the United States government, Fang-yi, the president of the Chinese Academy of Sciences, sent a delegation to visit the United States. It was composed of Zhou Peiyuan as leader, Qin Lisheng as deputy leader, Jiang Mingquan from the Chemistry Institute, Ma Dayou from the Acoustics Institute, Cheng Tso-hsin from the Zoology Institute and an interpreter. Four of them had studied in the US and had received their doctorates

169

there. On 17 April they flew from Beijing via Tokyo, San Fransisco and finally arrived in Washington. During the visit, meetings were held in the US Academy of Sciences. The Chinese delegation was invited to attend the closing ceremony and the dance which followed. The U S government arranged for the Chinese delegation to visit Washington DC during which they also saw the Washington Memorial, the Lincoln Memorial and the National Natural History Museum.

The National Natural History Museum is the largest and the most comprehensive natural history museum in the world. Founded in 1855 its collections are considerable, with the mineral specimens alone numbering about 18,000. Ten thousand drawers are full of specimens of human skeletons. There are many specimens from China too. All the specimens were kept in sealed cabinets made of iron or stainless steel, with automatic regulation of temperature and humidity, ventilators and other fixtures. Computers are used to catalogue the exhibits.

Even in the U S, Cheng could not forget his bird studies. One day he managed to find a collection of Chinese birds at Harvard University in Boston. Some of them had been gathered by an Englishman called La Touche from Guadun in Fujian province and were later sold to Harvard. Cheng was warmly welcomed by the Museum of Comparative Zoology of Harvard University where his friend, the world famous ornithologist, Dr E Mayr and his colleague, Dr Paynter held a banquet for him. In the afternoon, many posters appeared to announce a lecture on ornithology to be given by the Chinese professor, Cheng Tso-hsin.

After the dinner, Cheng began his lecture on ornithological research in China before an enormous crowd. His humorous words were very well received and although the lecture was due to end at about 8 o'clock the audience did not leave. They surrounded him to ask questions about the condition of the study of birds in China, and the specific sites of exploration there. Others asked about the political situation in China, as well as many other things about the country. Cheng answered everyone with great tolerance until nearly 11 o'clock when, fortunately, a Chinese of American nationality professor arrived to 'rescue' him.

It was midnight by the time Cheng returned to the hotel. The next day, he returned to Washington DC at

6am. The Chinese ambassador also went to the hotel to see the delegation. Cheng met many old friends in Washington and all four scientists wanted to revisit their former schools. With the permission of the U S government, Cheng went alone to Michigan University by plane. He found the department of biology from memory. But there was no one he knew there, not even the university dean, which was scarcely surprising as he had been away from the school for more than 50 years. And because he had not given any advance notice, there was no one to receive him there.

Dr G Archibald, director of the International Crane Foundation, invited Cheng to Baraboo in Wisconsin to visit the research centre for cranes which had recently been founded. Cheng arrived on 30 April and Dr Archibald met him at the airport and drove him to the centre himself. When the car reached the entrance to the centre, there was a brass band formed by students to welcome them. Cheng was very excited and gave an ebullient talk. Dr Archibald showed Cheng around his working place.

The ranch was very large and dozens of cranes were raised there. The centre was set up together by

Archibald and his schoolmate, Ron Sauey, whose father was a wealthy man and had raised horses there, and the abandoned horse ranch was used for raising cranes. They slept in the centre that night. Cheng was invited to the nearby Minniaji radio station to give a talk the next day.

On 2 May, Cheng went to Chicago to meet the delegation and visit the Field Museum of Natural History with them. The director of the Museum held a

Discussing with Dr George Archibald (director of the International Crane Foundation) at the International Conference on Cranes and Swans (January 1980, Hokkaida, Japan).

173

banquet of welcome at which Cheng was very happy to meet Dr Traylor, the expert on the silver pheasant. Dr Traylor especially invited Cheng to give a talk to the Bird Research Group and accommodated him at his own house that night. The next day, he drove Cheng to the nearby Nature Reserve and the National Park. When they talked about the new subspecies of the Emei silver pheasant, he said he admired Cheng very much and they became fast friends. The delegation returned to China on time after visiting Chicago. Everyone came back with fruitful results, including a large package of books and reference materials.

A second visit to the U S followed in September 1981. At that time the Chinese Federation for Science and Technology was going to the U S to discuss problems with the giant panda . Cheng was asked to be the head of the delegation and Wang Zheng one of the directors of the Federation, to be the vice-head. There were five other delegates. Because Cheng was busily engaged in ornithology, he tried hard to decline the invitation and suggested that experts studying mammals should go instead. But the Federation insisted on his going.

They arrived in Washington DC on 17 September. They went to the Smithsonian Institution the next day. The Institution had hoped to collaborate with their Chinese colleagues to study the giant panda. Although the clause about the insurance of the pandas put forward by the Chinese delegation was agreed by the Smithsonian Institution, lawyers thought that it was not consistent with US laws. The talks came to a deadlock.

Afterwards the U S government arranged for them to visit the National Park, the National Science Museum and the National Centre for the Protection and Research of Animals. The National Park is fairly grand, with hills, plains, and valleys and more than 3000 kinds of animals including some rare ones, such as the white tiger. In the park are green woods and lush and fragrant grass everywhere. There are bird laboratories, animal laboratories and some big bird houses in the park. They are not only for display but also for the scientific research carried on in the park.

In the National Museum, Cheng saw many collections and he discussed with the director of the bird division problems such as the identification of questionable specimens. The matter of several

175

different endangered animals from all over the world, such as David's deer from China, Arabia's long-horned grey antelope and some other rare species was raised in the National Centre for the Protection and Research of Animals. Indeed, this kind of raising and breeding base is an efficient measure of the recovery of endangered species. The equipment is very advanced and includes radio-tracking devices (suitable for the study of the large, middle-sized and small mammals as well as the birds), the automatic pickup cameras for the wild animals (with photo-electric reaction, photos are automatically taken when animals move), sound spectrograph (to analyse the sounds and behaviour of the animals), and all kinds of cages for trapping mammals.

On 20 September the delegation visited the Zoo belonging to the New York Zoological Society and the American Natural History Museum. The Zoo not only displays the animals but their environments. After you have visited the Zoo you feel that you have been travelling all around the world. There are exhibition halls for the diurnal animals and a small zoo especially designed for children, which imitates the animal habitats in a lively way and educates children at the same time. It is a great success. The comparative research of the Chinese alligators and the Mississippi crocodiles which are raised under controlled conditions are also a great success. The Natural History Museum has a long history and is one of the world's centres for the classification of birds. There are more than ten famous scholars in the museum. The number of bird specimens exceeds one million.

The Natural History Musem is the biggest in the U S. Cheng examined some of the specimens, especially those collected from China. He met the people in charge of the bird and mammal division and they exchanged academic information with each other. He also looked at some of the archaeological displays and the working places for the preparation of the animal specimens. During the talks, Cheng learned that work in the U S includes scientific projects from all over the world, such as the research on laughing thrushes and on bats. Much of the work involves the classification of some Chinese animals, so exchanging views was very beneficial for both sides.

On 23 September, the delegation went to Boston and visited Harvard University, the birthplace of U S ornithology. The famous ornithologists of those times, such as Agassiz, Audubon and Peters and taught and worked there; the list also includes Mayr who is still living and in good health.

Three days later he went to Pittsburgh to visit the Natural History Museum because Bing Zhi, one of the doyens in the Chinese zoological circle, who is now dead (1886-1965), had studied in the Carnegie research institutehere. There is an ecology research station attached to the Museum in the surburbs with an education division for teenagers and it provided accomodation for employees when they were on vacation or when they wrote papers. It was also used as the site for domestic and international academic conferences. The scientists there paid more attention to the ringing, netting, weighing, identifying and sexing of birds. Thousands of birds are ringed annually.

On 27 September, Cheng went to Ann Arbor from Pittsburgh and visited the University of Michigan again as well as the Animal Museum, the Natural Resource Department, the Study Centre of China and the International Institute for Exchange in the University. When the delegation arrived, the Chinese students in Michigan were holding a party to celebrate China's National Day. Mr Woodcock, the former American Ambassador to China, was a professor in Michigan at that time and he welcomed them enthusuastically. Mr Woodcock showed a keen interest in ornithology, and while working in China, he often invited Cheng to dinner and talked about birds. They enjoyed a firm friendship. The University this time held a grand ceremony for Cheng. By permission of the board of trustees, the president of the University, Dr Harold T Shapiro presented Cheng with a Certificate of Merit for Science. Those who took part included besides ex-Ambassador Woodcock, professors of the department of zoology and the Chinese students in Michigan. News of the ceremony was published in the university magazine and in the local newspapers the next day.

On 30 September, the delegation flew to San Fransisco to visit the Academy of Science of the University of California/Berkeley. The Academy concentrates its efforts on collecting animals and birds of the western areas in the US. There were also many specimens from north-east China. The devices for studying the birds' sounds and the aquariums there

An honorary scientific award conferred by the University of Michigan, USA. On the right is Dr H T Shapiro, president of the university and on the left is Prof L Woodcock, a former American ex-ambassador to China.

180

were remarkable. Berkeley is one of the best colleges in the U S and its scientific research in every field is famous around the world. In the Museum there are a good many samples of wild mammal chromosomes preserved and the original records drawn from long-term field investigation, which is the only one of this kind among all the U S research institutes. The research of the bird's protein electrophoresis in Berkeley is well known too.

When the delegation visited Berkeley they met Ms Yu Liqing who came from Taiwan and was studying in Berkeley at that time. At first she wanted to be an interpreter, but after meeting the delegation she found that most of them could speak good English, so she accomapanied them to every laboratory and explained in Chinese, often saying, "we are all Chinese." When she learned the head of our team was Cheng Tso-hsin, she exclaimed: "When I studied at University in Taiwan, we used the textbook written by Prof Cheng!" When the delegation arrived in San Fransciso, there were many parties being held by overseas Chinese to celebrate Chinese National Day. At the Chinese consulate in San Francisco, Cheng met with the consul Hu Dingyi, who had worked in the Chinese

Embassy in Britain. He held a tea party for them to celebrate China's National Day. Cheng asked Hu Dingyi if he could invite his American friends who helped him so much in the U S and Hu Dingyi agreed with great pleasure.

In San Fransisco, Cheng was encouraged by his relatives to visit the Red Wood Park and the Yellowstone Nature Reserve. The Red Wood Park lies in the middle of California and it was founded in 1864. It is a valley with precipitous rocks, big Chinese larches, magnificent waterfalls, dark green lakes and shining rivers. Its beautiful scenery enjoys a great reputation in the USA. In order to prevent timber merchants from wantonly cutting the Chinese larches, a law was passed by Congress in 1864 which put the valley under national administration. President Lincoln announced that the valley and the Manieposhaju woods, several kilometres away, "could only be used for public entertainment and no buying or selling of its land was to be permitted." It was the first law laid down to preserve natural scenery in the world.

The Yellowstone National Park lies in the north-west of Wyoming and attracts some 200,000 visitors annually. Cheng had visited it in the 1940s. No other place around the world possesses warmer springs, the most magnificent being the numerous intermittent springs. The most famous geyser 'Old Faithful' spouts every 33 to 96 minutes and lasts four to five minutes each time. The burning hot water spurts into the high sky to meet with cold air to form a mist which rises to considerable heights. The colourful steam looks very beautiful. There are also more than 200 black bears and more than 10,000 big-horned deer in the park. The smaller birds and beasts are even more bountiful and of great variety.

Although the delegation did not succeed in reaching an agreement in these talks, it improved China's knowledge of the U S and benefitted the extension of the knowledge of science and technology. And it also furthered the mutual friendship between the Chinese and the United States people.

* * * * * *

1980 was a busy year for Cheng Tso-hsin. He attended several conferences. In January he went to Japan, in

April he flew to the United States, in May he attended the International Symposium of the Investigation of the Qinghai-Tibet Plateau in Beijing, in September he went to Japan again and in October he was invited to lead a Chinese delegation to Australia to attend the annual meeting of the Museums in Sydney. Other members included Zhang Wensong, the vice director of Beijing Museum and three scientists from Beijing, Tianjin and Shanghai.

On 6 October the China Ornithological Society was founded in Dalian, Liaoning province. Cheng was one of the founders of the Society and attended its first conference. He made a speech at the opening ceremony in the morning and presented a paper in the afternoon. In the evening, he returned to Beijing to go through the formalities for going abroad and to prepare a speech and to pack his luggage. On 11 October he left Beijing for Sydney via Tokyo. At that time, Cheng was already 74. He was old but very energetic. He went from one country to another without stopping, just like a diplomat. He went to visit America (as described in the previous chapter) again after returning from Australia! In fact, Cheng had suffered from hypertension since the 1960s and had

Reception sponsored by Dr Y Yamashina (director of the Yamashina Institute of Ornithology) in Tokyo, Japan 1980.

some trouble with his heart as well. But all he thought about was his career, a strong stimulant encouraging him to work and disregard his tiredness.

Sydney is the largest city and the biggest port in Australia. Both the University of Sydney and Sydney Museum were the first to be founded in the country. The Sydney Pagoda, 3,048 metres high and the highest building in the southern hemisphere, is a round building, four stories underground and 47 stories above the ground, with a rotating observation restaurant at the top. The annual meeting was held in

185

a conference hall of this building. On behalf of the Chinese delegation, Cheng made a speech and presented a model of the skull fossil of the 'Peking Man' as a gift to the conference.

The delegation was invited to visit the Coral Island in the nearby sea by helicopter. There were many different kinds of coral on the Island and some of them were dazzlingly brilliant. Cheng had only seen pictures of coral in his middle school textbooks and in

Professor Cheng with Fang Yi (President of the Chinese Academy of Sciences) in the International Symposium on the Qinghai-Xizang (Tibet) Plateau May 24 - June 1, Beijing.

186

Sydney he saw the real thing which made a great impression. Then the delegation visited the Taronga Park where there are many rare and endemic species of birds and mammals, all very different from the animals in China. The emu is a good example. It is a large bird, as tall as a human, with a sharp beak and two strong feet on which to run very fast. It often approaches tourists aggressively.

After visiting the Park, the delegation went to north Australia to see field research on the bower bird. The bower bird inhabits the shrubbery in woodlands. During the breeding season, it builds a bower with grass, roots and twigs of trees, supported by thicker, young branches, and ornamented with lichens, flowers and fresh grass on the outside, and sometimes there is even a second storey. The nests are hung on a tree at another site far from the bower. These special breeding habits and characteristics differ greatly from those of any other bird. The delegation was very interested to see them.

After visiting north Australia, the delegation went south. They reached Canberra, the capital of Australia, where the buildings were designed by an American architect following the model of Washington. In the centre of the city lies Congress

Hall, surrounded by roads to every direction. All the buildings in the city are arranged in perfect order. When the delegation arrived, a ministry delegation received them and the Friendship Union also gave a banquet in their honour before they went on to Melbourne. There are many overseas Chinese there and they gave a welcoming party. After the speech given by the local Chinese, Cheng gave an academic report which attracted everyone's interest. The party was very jolly.

During their visit to Melbourne, a trip was organised to Baltarat to see the famous gold mine there. Discovered after the San Fransisco gold mine, the gold there has now been exploited completely. At a museum of gold mining, the minerals displayed provided a detailed description of the history and production of the mine to which Chinese workers had made a tremendous contribution. At that time the Chinese workers did all the hard and rough work, and they were famous for their tolerance. There is a Guangong temple near the mine and many Chinese workers went there annually to offer sacrifices to Guangong (an ancient Chinese hero who was very loyal to his friends) or to their ancestors. They admired Guangong, as if he was their spirits' mainstay He united everyone and helped the expatriate Chinese to set up the Overseas Chinese Organization to help each other and deal with their difficulties together. When the delegation arrived, the overseas Chinese entertained them with sumptuous Guangdong dishes. They still retain a lot of Chinese traditions, customs and habits.

They flew from Melbourne, passing Adelaide and Perth and had a short rest in Thailand before going on to Hong Kong. In Hong Kong Cheng's students and friends came to meet him and they told him that he had been elected president of the China Ornithological Society. Cheng felt surprised, because he had only attended the meeting for its foundation one day before he had gone abroad. The delegation brought back many books and data about the large museums in Australia. The trip had been very useful indeed.

What Cheng Tso-hsin had done also helped China to make friends in the world and extend the influence of the Chinese.

Cheng Tso-hsin was always very honest when undertaking his official duties and always made a clear distinction between public and private interests.

In the 1980s he had visited the former Soviet Union twice, receiving the excellent remuneration of a Russian professor. When he returned to China, he bought instruments and translator radios for the Institute of Zoology with the foreign exchange he had saved in the Soviet Union (at that time his family only possessed a portable radio). In 1978 he had been to France and Britain for two months. To save money, he did not eat in the hotel restaurant but had instead bought bread, milk, fruit and sausages in nearby markets to feed himself. In this way he saved over £1000. When he came back, he only took out some of the money to show his family what pounds looked like. "Our country is not rich now. It is not easy to have this foreign currency. Although we saved it, it should be used where it is needed badly" he told them. On the following day he handed every coin back to the Institute.

In 1981 he went abroad as a member of scientific delegation sponsored by the Chinese government, so he had the privilege of passing through the customs without being examined. However, he did not bring back anything for his family except a small recorder given by his relatives overseas, although he did bring back a number of documents and books for his

Institute. His children felt somewhat disappointed when meeting him at the airport. Cheng Huaijie, his eldest son, described their mood later in a short essay entitled *The precious gift father brought back*: "Father, over 70 years old, was returning to Beijing after completing a scientific investigation abroad. It happened to be a holiday and the Institute had sent a car to collect him. We were so eager to meet him that all our family, ten people from three generations, all got into the car to the airport. The plane arrived and there were so many people carrying a lot of big and small cases passing through customs. This time, we thought father would have brought some foreign goods for us. His grandson was looking forward especially. Look! Here was my old father and his young assistant. We skipped and jumped with joy when he came out of customs to embrace him. After a while, his luggage was sent to the examination room by automatic conveyor belt and we helped to take it away. We all love him, especially his grandson. On returning back home, my mother asked, 'What is in all this luggage?' Father answered proudly that there were instruments and books which the Institute needed badly. He bought them with the money he had

191

put aside from his allowance and the income of his academic exchanges. Only in Hong Kong had he used some of the money to buy two tapes for our younger brother to study English. That was all! Though she understood father, my mother was still worried that the children were disappointed, especially her grandson. Finally, my mother made him give the key chain presented him in the plane to their grandson as a gift to pacify him.

"Before the Cultural Revolution my father had gone abroad many times. But every time it was the same. On one occasion he went to east Germany to attend an academic meeting. He brought back a set of high grade telescopes and a radio, but they were for his Institute. He said the money had been from public funds, therefore the goods should belong to the public. Unforturnately, nobody knows where these goods went during the Cultural Revolution. Father has devoted 60 years to scientific research and education. He is always meticulous in his scholarship, regarding his undertaking as more important than his life and even more important than money. He has not brought any family electrical appliances back from abroad, not because they are not needed by his family, but because he thought that he should not buy them with the saved foreign exchange. Once he saved many pounds while working in Britain and it was reasonable for him to keep them. But he handed them back to the Institute where he worked. From father I appreciated the noble instinct to help China. That is why he has achieved great success in his field. We learned this kind of spirit again on this occasion. This is indeed a precious gift father brought back to us."

Cheng handed all the foreign exchange he had saved to the country. And he often uses his own salary and allowances to prepare family banquets for foreign guests visiting him at home with his family. Once, when an officer from the Institute came to Cheng's home to discuss something he found Cheng entertaining foreign visitors. The officer said "The money is spent on work, so it should be reimburised to you in accordance with the rules." But Cheng insisted on not doing that. Welcoming foreign guests warmly and discussing academic topics not only broadened his knowledge but also provided advantages to his research work. So Cheng and his wife are ready to do anything beneficial to help the causes they are undertaking.

EDITING AND TEACHING

In the early years of the new China, a council meeting of the China Zoological Society was held in Beijing in June of 1951 to make national plans for zoological research. At the meeting all members agreed that China was rich in animal resources, and that some research work had been done by colleges and academic organisations. But we had neither united research nor even uniform terms. The founding of the new China provided us with the opportunity to

Loving Bird Conference sponsored by the Science and Technology Commission of the State Council in the Reclining-Budda Temple, Beijing in April 1986.

194

mobilise all forces and to organise the work. So the council decided that the zoological workers concerned should compile an atlas of animals which were economic, endemic and academically important in line with their priorities. With a brief description attached to each animal plate we would have a consensus in scientific research and education to promote the development of zoological research and the spreading of knowledge about animals.

At that time, Cheng Tso-hsin took charge of the edition of the *Atlas of Chinese Birds* which was the first step of the national plan. Two volumes of *Distribution List of Chinese Birds* were published in 1955 and 1955. The first and second volumes of *Atlas of Chinese Birds* published in 1959 attracted much attention from zoological workers. The two volumes were combined into one for the second edition in 1966 and they were soon out of stock. Copies of the third edition, in 1987 were also sold out as soon as published. From this you can see how they were needed. On 1 June 1962, the Chinese Academy of Sciences set up the editorial board for *Fauna Sinica*. This consisted of 12 members including Cheng. They were Wang Jiaji (protozoa), Liu Chengjiao (reptiles),

Wu Xianwen (fish), Shou Zhenghuang (mammals), Cheng Tso-hsin (birds), Chen Xintao (parasites), Chen Shixiang (insects), Bing Zhi (invertebrates), Liu Zhiying (insects), Zhang Xi (molluscs), Tong Dizhou (vertebrates) and Yang Weiyi (insects). However, most of them did not survive the Cultural Revolution. Up to 1980, the editorial board re-engaged over 30 members for increasing the editorial strength. The *Fauna Sinica* consisted of three sections, vertebrates, invertebrates and insects.

Birds (*Aves*) belong to the section of vertebrates. *Avifauna Sinica* was planned to consist of 14 volumes. The work covers all the species of birds so far known in China. For each species, the following topics were covered: scientific nomenclature, identification characteristics, description, discussion of taxonomic problems (if any), differentiation of sub-species, ecology, distribution and economic significance. It not only summarises results of faunal studies and achievements, but also helps to push forward a more thorough and intensive investigation of all the birds throughout a big and marvellous country like China.

Being an editor of *Avifauna Sinica*, Cheng energetically undertook, with the cooperation of his colleagues all the editorial tasks, although he realised that it would take a long time to complete the 14 volumes. In order to meet the needs of the time, he managed to compile the *Economic Birds of China* in 1963. This book includes 241 species of birds which belong to 18 orders and 56 families. There are systematic keys throughout and it also deals with hunting, husbandary, development and utilisation of bird resources as well as bird pests with control measures. Generally it provided systematic scientific material for future research and the utilisation of resourceful birds. The book was well received.

The American Commercial Department translated it into English and made it into minature films for wide distribution. In fact, the publication of this book provided a good foundation for *Avifauna Sinica*. In 1978, just after the Cultural Revolution, Cheng added to and revised some of the contents of *Distribution List of Chinese Birds*, and it was reprinted. This indicated a new stage of the *Avifauna Sinica*.

In order to meet the needs of international exchange, Cheng was asked by the Chinese Science

Press and Paul Parey Scientific Publishers to compile the book as a synopsis of the *Avifauna of China* in English. It was published in 1987, excellently printed and with clear illustrations. It contains 1.2 million letters and 1,224 pages. Because of the limited number of copies, it is very difficult to obtain now.

This book lists all the known birds in China up to the end of 1982 including 1,186 species and 593 subspecies, breeding habitats and current status. Compared with the *Distribution List of Chinese Birds* also written by Cheng, it includes an additional 20 species and 44 subspecies and adds information on breeding habitats and current status. Up to now, it is the most comprehensive account of the birds of China and is also the first to summarise completely and systematically a whole animal class in China. It provides not only the essential basis for contemporary ornithological study, but also all the available data on China's birds for world ornithology. According to scientific statistics issued in 1980, there were 9,021 species of birds all over the world, of which 1,186 species were found in China (1982). The number is almost equal to the sum of bird species in Europe and in Australia. American has only about 770 species and

Lecturing to post-graduate students in the Institute of Zoology (1980).

Japan fewer than 510 species. The former Soviet Union has a larger territory but fewer bird species than China.

China is a country rich in birds. But before you know thoroughly the resource status, it is better to hold your tongue. You can see from this what an important role *A Synopsis of the Avifauna of China* plays.

This book deals with classification, systematics, subspecific differentiation, ecology, distribution, breeding habitat and present status for a whole class of vertebrates (*Aves*) in China. It offers scientific data, which are of use in the studies of bird migration, bird conservation, and ornithological regionalization as well as in the formulation of wildlife decrees and game laws.

After publication, Cheng's *Synopsis* received high praise in European and American ornithological journals and periodicals. In 1989, the book was awarded the first-class prize for natural science by the Chinese Academy of Sciences and the second-class prize for natural science by the National Com mission of Science and Technology. In addition, the scientific committee of the Chinese Academy of Sciences awarded Cheng a medal.

On 26 May 1989, the banquet hall of Beijing's five-star Shangrila Hotel was ablaze with lights. More than 100 people, including many eminent people - Song Jian, the chairman of the National Commission of Science and Technology, Cheng Siyuan, vice president of Chinese People's Political Consultative Conference, the president of the Chinese Academy of Sciences, the director of the Institute of Zoology attended the award ceremony. At the reception, Cheng was awarded the American National Wildlife

Federation Special Conservation Achievement in 1989. Prof Cheng was introduced on the invitation card as follows: "Man's understanding of the animal kingdom has been greatly enriched by Professor Cheng Tso-hsin's dedication to the field of ornithology. Founder and President of the China Zoological Society and the China Ornithological Society, Professor Cheng Tso-hsin's work during the past 50 years includes discovering 15 new sub-species of Chinese birds. While the scores of scientific books, papers and articles he has authored have been mostly in Chinese, his most recent work, *A synopsis of the Avifauna of China*, is in English. The 1224-page volume covers all the birds discovered and recorded in China. Considered a pioneer in developing a systematic study of birds in China, Professor Cheng is the leading expert in his country. Respected internationally for his knowledge, he has assisted researchers around the world by examining bird specimens in museums and universities in the United States, England, France, Germany and the Soviet Union. A graduate of the University of Michigan, Professor Cheng today serves as research professor of ornithology at the Institute of Zoology of the Chinese

Academy of Sciences in Beijing. President of the World Pheasant Association and adviser to the International Crane Foundation, Professor Cheng is also a corresponding member of the British, German and American Ornithological Societies, and an honorary fellow with the latter."

Professor Cheng, then 83 years old, walked up to the rostrum and received the medal and trophy accompanied by his wife, Ms Chen Jia-jian to the warm applause of the audience. Dr Jay D Hair, president of National Wildlife Federation, said that this was an award for Dr Cheng's remarkable contribution to ornithological research in China over 50 years. It is the first time that the Federation has awarded a Chinese scholar and also the first time the reception has been held outside America. In his answering speech, Cheng expressed his thanks and pleasure, and then went on to emphasise that all his achievements were due to the leadership of the Chinese Communist Party, especially the reform and opening-up policy, and the support and assistance from other biological researchers.

At the banquet table, Mr Song Jian said to Cheng "Prof Cheng, the Communist Party and people of

A special conservation achievement award conferred on Professor Cheng by the National Wildlife Federation of USA. The reception was sponsored by Dr Jay D Hair, president of the Federation for Cheng's whole family on 26 May 1989 in Beijing, China.

China thank you for making such a speech under such circumstances. Thank you for your belief in the Party and support for it."

In 1993, Cheng revised *Economic Birds of China* according to the Law of Wildlife Conservation of China. This time he added the results of all the latest research over the past 20 years, as well as many new opinions and viewpoints. For example, he clarified further the roles birds played in the national economic life of the nation, realising that birds' indirect effects might be more important than direct ones in controlling damage caused by rates, mice and injurious insects. Birds are an essential part of nature and an important factor in maintaining the ecological balance. We must regard them as our friends and protect them. We can use them legally, lastingly and reasonably as long as we protect them. Only in this way can we make full use of bird resources not only for our generation but for future generations as well. In fact the revised edition stated Dr Cheng's views on the three measures necessary to conserve wildlife: protection, captive breeding and habitat preservation.

The first is protection. Which species of wildlife should we select to protect? Cheng thought we should protect the endangered species first, such as *Nipponia nippon*. In the meantime, we should also raise such species artificially. There are many kinds of endemic species of birds in China, such as brown eared-pheasants, golden pheasants and Cabot's tragopan. There are many useful and beneficial birds in China. We should protect the beneficial birds to make them reproduce more and more to meet the needs of people better. Lastly, in protecting our ecological environment, we should preserve favourable habitats for birds, such as forests for pheasants and wetlands for waterfowl.

* * * * * *

China is famous for her vast territory, rich resources and the variety of landscapes and different climates. There are very many species of birds and mammals; 1,186 species and 953 sub-species of birds alone have already been identified. Compared to the abundance of birds, however, the number of bird researchers is very small. China now has only over 100 professional ornithologists and especially since the Cultural Revolution, not enough have been considered as qualified.

Cheng Tso-hsin, even though he is 88, still supervises doctorate and post-doctorate students. Over the past decades he has brought up scores of graduate students, recommended students and postgraduate students to major in ornithology, helped them to decide on research projects and guided them as to how to conduct field investigations, collect specimens and ecological data, and what references to read. In addition he has given them lectures, supervised their studies, examined paper and even corrected their English to help them to improve their ability to write papers in English.

Most of his postgraduate students have become associate professors, professors, and first class researchers. They are distributed throughout the country as well as overseas making up a corps of Chinese bird researchers.

Cheng believes that although it is very important to train specialists by college education, the number is too limited to meet the needs of bird study.

So he has paid much attention to amateur enthusiasts and selected some competent ones to study further in order to expand the bird research team. Over the years some bird enthusiasts have sent

Talking about Chinese birds to young people at the Youngsters Palace, Beijing, June 1983.

their manuscripts to Cheng asking for his advice. He has always revised them word by word, and written back to answer their questions. Even in hospital, he would ask his children to write back for him.

Ju Xijiang, a young bird enthusiast from Shanxi province, has communicated with Cheng for more than 30 years. He and his wife visited his venerable teacher just before the Spring Festival in 1993 when they were visiting Beijing on business. Cheng has also established contact with many other amateurs including students, teachers in primary schools and middle schools, doctors, cadres and workers. Three middle school students from Wu Meng mountainous region of Yunnan province, Song Yao, Tang Yuping and Liu Qing, took part in spare-time bird research in 1980, after which they could identify more than 300 species and collected more than 1000 specimens. Two of them later carried out zoological work in the western part of Yunnan and wanted to take part in ornithological research. They wrote to Cheng to let him know what they were doing; Cheng wrote back to encourage them to study hard to lay a solid base for future work. When he later discovered their progress in bird research, he was very heartened. Cheng always thought that the number of bird researchers was too few and that more would be needed for the future. So he always treated generously those who had persecuted him during the Cultural Revolution. He never looked down on anybody who realised their mistakes and could correct them. If it was to the benefit of bird research he would put them to work, even in important positions, despite their past. Cheng's motto is: 'The significance of one's life is the devotedness to one's enterprise, not to be remorseful to our ancestors or descendants.'

There is ample evidence that Cheng is full of hope and love for the young. We must start with the young children throughout the nation to improve their scientific and technological minds and encourage their appreciation of birds. Of this Cheng is sure.

In 1983, he was invited to the summer camp in Jinshan mountain organised by the Beijing Children's Palace. Sitting happily beside the camp fire, he explained the difference between birds such as a kite and an eagle. In 1984, Cheng was invited by the Beijing Children's Palace to talk about birds at the meeting of Beijing Youth Bird-Loving Week. The elementary school students listened attentively to the stories about birds and the various specimens he had in his hands. Not a sound could be heard except Cheng's voice or, from time to time, loud laughter. When he had finished there was loud applause and many children went to the rostrum to look at the specimens more carefully and to hear more about birds from their 'grandpa'.

In April of 1986, Beijing's Bird Meeting organised by the Chinese Commission of Science and Technology in the People's Great Hall attracted approximately 10,000 people. At the meeting Cheng gave a lecture on 'Loving Birds'. He held it as his responsibility to popularize scientific knowledge among the masses. In May 1992, he was invited to take part in the Festival of Science and Technology at which some outstanding primary school students were to be honoured. At that time Cheng had just come out of hospital after about eight months because of heart illness. The doctors would not allow him to go to parties and his family also tried to persuade him to send a congratulatory message to the meeting rather than attend it. But he insisted on going, accompanied by his wife.

The teachers and students gave a warm welcome to them and seeing 'Rehabilitating Sparrows' written on a blackboard, he smiled. He felt even happier when he saw the biological specimens, teaching materials and articles produced by the teachers and students in the exhibition room. Ge Shouxi, the headmistress, showed him a specimen of a grey heron which had collided with the plane her son was trying to land at Hang Zhou - a case of bird strike. The dead bird was subsequently found and preserved. Cheng announced that bird strike was a new Darwin's problem. He gave three books to the school. *The Theory of Evolution* translated by him, *Atlas of Chinese Birds* and *The Rare and Precious Animals in China* and made a spontanous speech. He said, "I would suggest three points for your consideration. The first is to have a real faith in and for our motherland. The second is to work really hard, love your work, and dedicate yourself to it. The third is work in a thoroughly realistic way according to the needs of the country". He said that the three points were his philosophy and work. He hoped that it would also be so for the students. This was broadcasted by Beijing Radio and printed in the *Beijing Evening News* and *Beijing Daily* to reflect their respect for the old scientist's attention to and hope for young people.

In order to encourage more young to devote themselves to ornithological study and to develop the cause of research in China, Cheng contributed the cash prize he had won for his book *A Synopsis of the Avifauna of China* (English version) and the other cash prizes he received from the Chinese Academy of Sciences and the Chinese Commission of Science and Technology to establish The Cheng Tso-hsin's Award

Foundation for Young Ornithologists.

The Award was set up to reward young researchers who have obtained outstanding achievements in bird research. A management committee of the Foundation has been established which consists of five leading Chinese ornithologists recommended by the China Ornithological Society. Professor Zheng Guangmei, the president of the Society, was elected as chairman of the committee. The prize will be awarded once every two years from 1994 to two or three young ornithologists. The regulations for the Foundation have been published. The Cheng Foundation would like to receive donations, either from China or from abroad. It has already attracted much attention and support from the colleagues and amateurs involved in bird research worldwide.

MISCELLANY

Cheng Tso-hsin considered that, to encourage appreciation of birds, we could learn from other countries which had selected a 'National Bird' as their symbol. This would combine bird conservation with the patriotism and enhance bird consciousness. In 1983 Cheng wrote an article entitled *Talking about the National Birds* for the *Beijing Evening Newspaper* which was subsequently choosen as an excellent article in the 'Scientific Corridor' column of that newspaper. In it Cheng introduced the concept of 'National Birds', pointing out that birds have colourful plumage and a beautiful body shape. They are tame and have attractive calls. They have been studied more thoroughly and scientifically than any other class of animal. Since birds are liked by human beings, and are discussed by them more than other animals, there arises a problem of which species is the most popular.

If people of a certain area are keen on one bird it should be adopted as a 'Local Bird', 'County Bird' or 'Province Bird' the same way as in a country, where people select the most popular bird as their 'National Bird'.

The idea of a 'National Bird' originated in the USA. In 1782, the bald eagle *Haliaeetus leucocrephalus* nearly became extinct. In order to save it and make Americans more conservation conscious, Congress decided that the bald eagle should be the 'National Bird'. In 1872, the resplendent quetzal *Pharomachrus mocinno* was selected to be the 'National Bird'. in Vedimala, because it has beautiful plumage and was preferred by local people. The green pheasant *Phasianus versicolor* is a popular bird which appears frequently in the fairy tales of Japan and such was the attraction for it that the Japanese decided that it should be adopted as their 'National Bird' in 1947. The Eurasian robin *Erithacus rubecula* has a lovely song, feeds mainly on pests, and is much enjoyed by the British, who call it The Bird of God. In 1960, the robin was selected by ballot to be the 'National Bird'.

In the Netherlands the white spoonbill *Platelea leucorodia* is a famous fish hunter. People there love it and call it a Fisherbird. It is also the 'National Bird'. The barn swallow *Hirundo rustica* is a good pest catcher and the people of Estonia and Austria selected it as their 'National Bird'.

China with 1243 species and 944 sub-species recorded up to 1992 is rich in birds. If people who are so keen on birds want to select a 'National Bird', we should consider 1) an endemic bird of China; 2) an endangered bird; 3) a species with sound economic value; 4) a species benefitting agriculture, forestry and animal husbandry; 5) a bird which has a special relationship with the culture and history of China; 6) a bird with colourful plumage and a lovely call.

Cheng agreed that the selection of a 'National Bird' should attract the interests of all Chinese people and should be decided by due procedure, within a certain period of time. This would enhance the bird consciousness of Chinese people to a new level.

In 1992, the China Ornithological Society decided that the golden pheasant *Chrysolophus pictus* should be the symbol of the society and Cheng expressed his approval. The golden pheasant is an endemic species of considerable size and with colourful plumage which shows the magnificent features of our great country and symbolises the flourishing development of our economy. The golden pheasant is also rare in China and needs protection and captive breeding. This bird was first found in Shanxi province, in an area

215

called 'Baoji county' (Chinese for "treasure pheasant county") by local people. It was also introduced to Europe in the eighteenth century. Cheng had also made up his mind to study birds because of his admiration for this wonderful bird. He hopes that it will be the 'National Bird' of China, symbolising our country's development into a prosperous and strong 'Treasure Pheasant' country.

* * * * * *

In spring 1992, as part of its contribution to Bird Appreciation Week, *Forestry News*, published by the Ministry of Forestry, held a competition about ornithological knowledge among its readers. Most of the questions were familiar to Cheng Tso-hsin's family because they often discussed them. His family thought that they could easily answer all the questions with Cheng's advise. But to their surprise, when they checked the answers with him, he forbade them to enter the competition because he thought it would be unfair. Cheng's attitude was beyond the comprehension of his sons and grandsons. Why didn't grandfather allow them to take part? He had such a close association with birds that he couldn't live for a day without them around him. Was he afraid that they couldn't answer the questions correctly? If not, surely grandpa could give them the correct answer. But it was because they could answer the questions that Cheng wanted them not to enter.

This episode reflects Cheng's ethics. Although he has studied birds for decades, he has never displayed a single bird specimen in his house. Is it because he doesn't love them? Of course not! Or is it because the specimens are not worthy of being displayed? Again no. Isn't he able to obtain valuable or rare specimens? Of course not; if he wanted, he could get specimens from researchers all over the country, or even keep for himself specimens given by foreign friends. But he has never collected bird specimens for himself.

For Cheng argued that if he displayed various bird specimens in his house it would be taken that he could not distinguish between public and private life. If he put the specimens in his house, some people would say that it was just because his profession was ornithological research. He would like to be like the experts who don't collect and keep cultural objects for themselves, though they are specialists in identifying them. It is occupational ethics. Cheng has kept in close touch with colleagues at home and abroad, friends and relatives, by way of letters. His children often write them for him. He always tells them, again and again, not to use his official headed paper and envelopes for private purposes.

During the Spring Festival of 1992, a German engineer brought a specimen of an eagle owl to Cheng's home. It was very beautiful, with its wings extended. His sons and grandsons wanted to display it in their home but they knew that Cheng wouldn't allow them to do so. So they asked if they could display it only for a few days during the holidays. But Cheng said that it should be sent to the Institute as soon as possible, insisting no matter how much they argued. Finally his wife, who understood him best persuaded the children to take the specimen to the Institute of Zoology along with her.

As an ornithological specialist, Cheng never kept a living bird in his home. But in the 1950s he did raise a sparrow in his house in order to calculate its capacity for food. In that time, food for humans was limited, so he fed the sparrow with his own. However, he mixed the public with private this time because he thought it could and should be so. After the Cultural Revolution, Cheng began to raise birds, such as parrots and song birds, in cages for two reasons. First, they were ornamental birds raised artificially and not wild, so they were not protected. Second, it benefits bird care and appreciation.

The campaign to love and protect birds all over the country is a fight against seizing and killing wild birds, on keeping caged birds instead of catching wild birds. If you visit him now, you will find several pairs of white song birds raised in light green cages hung in front of the windows which his wife feeds everyday. Their beautiful songs always attract the attention of guests.

There has been a most important rule in Cheng's family for past decades: there is nothing more important than causes. Cheng Huaijie, his eldest son, graduated from high school and was admitted to Beijing Steel & Iron College. At that time, middle school teachers were scarce in Beijing. So the government mobilised the best graduates to remain in middle schools working as teachers. Being a leader of the Youth League at the school, Cheng Huaijie wanted to be a teacher but when he consulted with his parents,

Cheng said, "It should be decided by yourself" because he knew clearly that a youth should meet the needs of the society and serve it.

Supported by his parents, Cheng Huaijie became a middle school teacher. He has now been working at the school for 40 years. He was promoted to the position of a leader of the school in 1960 because of his excellent work but was criticised and denounced during the Cultural Revolution. After the Revolution, he was appointed to be headmaster. A journalist once interviewed him at a commemorative reception at the Beijing Education Bureau in October 1988 and asked him what he thought about his work. Cheng Huaijie said "I have no complains and regrets about what I have done".

The journalist published an article in *Beijing Daily* on 23 April 1989 showing Cheng Huaijie's achievements. Cheng Huaijie has devoted almost all his life to general education. The National Education Committee and the China Central TV produced a TV series entitled *Royalty* before Teachers' Day 1991. Cheng Huaijie's achievement was shown in the first episode called *Desiring*. He believed that he could not have achieved anything without the help and support, both spiritual and material, of his parents. Cheng Huaijing, the second son, was sent to a bearing factory in a mountain valley of Ningxia in north-west China to work as a doctor after he graduated from Beijing Medical College. His parents supported him while he worked in the the remote areas. Cheng Huaijing did an excellent job in the factory hospital, carrying out many surgical operations and saving many patients.

He worked in Ningxia for eight years and it was not until he had passed the entrance examination for registering as a postgraduate that he returned to Beijing. During the wave of going abroad, Cheng Huaijing also wanted to go to the United States to continue his studies. Although he had many contacts overseas, Cheng said "If I recommend anybody, I would like to recommend my young colleagues and students of the Zoological Institute rather than my own children".

Cheng has indeed written to recommend many scientists to go abroad. He recommended his graduate student, Lu Taichun, to study in England, Wang Xiangting, Li Xiangtao, He Fenqi and some other researchers to England, Liu Rushun to Thailand, Ding Wen-ning, Xu Yangong to America to attend an academic conference. But he hasn't recommended his own children to go abroad to study. Cheng's children understood their father. They went abroad to broaden their professional knowledge all by themselves. Cheng Huaijing was sent to France by his hospital to attend an academic meeting. Cheng Huaiming, his eldest daughter, visited Japan as the deputy director of Tianjin Technology Supervision Bureau.

The relationship within the family is democratic and equal. Before his birthday in November 1992, Cheng received a letter of 9000 wishes from his eldest daughter-in-law, who was in the south. Cheng wrote back to her saying "I am very glad to receive your letter of congratulation. However, you didn't point out my shortcomings. I know I have many and hope you will mention them in future so I can correct them. It is so precious to me that I will keep the letter forever." This letter embodied the relationship between two generations in the family. The parents take a great deal of care of the everyday lives for their chilrdren.

Cheng Huaijie and his wife have three children. Being very busy they have never accompanied their children to hospital or attended parent-teacher meetings from primary to middle school. All of these were done by Chen Jia-jian. She said "Go to work and concentrate on your jobs. I will help you look after the children."

The rebels said that it was exploiting to hire a baby-sitter during the Cultural Revolution and Cheng was forced to dismiss the old baby-sitter who had been working for the family for more than 30 years. At that time, Cheng's youngest grandson was only four years old. In order to let the family members get to work on time, Cheng himself took and collected his grandson from kindergarten for several months. Cheng's two sons worked outside Beijing, so Cheng and his wife took care of their children in Beijing. Because of their love for their children, they in return respect and care for their parents very much. So do their grandsons. Because Cheng could not walk easily due to age, his children bought a special stick for him, a magnifying glass for him to read more easily and a soft chair for him to sit in. In a word, they did what their father wouldn't think doing for himself. So Cheng wrote in a letter to his eldest daughter-in-law "what makes me happy is that all my children are so kind to me. Our family is the best family in the world." A harmonious and comfortable family is very important to old men who live a healthy and long life.

223

When he was a small boy, Cheng Tso-hsin loved nature and liked to explore its mysteries. Perhaps this stimulated him to become an ornithologist. In addition he had many hobbies: when he studied in America he liked to play tennis, and watch football matches. After he returned to Fujian Christian University, he often played tennis with his students or his wife. Tennis played an important part in his love for his wife so they kept the pair of rackets brought back from America. He also played bridge and chess at weekends. Before the Cultural Revolution he often played the piano and in the 1950s, went to dances with his wife at weekends.

He also liked to collect stamps. He was once president of the Stamp-Collectors Society of the Chinese Academy of Science and is now its honorary president. He has particular views about stamp-collecting. He regards it as beneficial because you can broaden your views, understand the political and cultural evolution and development of many countries, refresh yourself after hard work and make friends. Collecting stamps can promote the cultural exchange among researchers and make people make more of their lives. Furthermore, like scientific research, it demands the collection and analysis of data of various kinds of stamps, cultivating the habits and abilities to assess, classify and analyse. Thus Cheng thinks that stamp-collecting is a good hobby for scientific workers.

Cheng reached the view about the relationship between stamp-collecting and scientific research from his own experience, in that the collection, classification and research of stamps is associated with the collection, identification and research of birds. He regards stamp-collecting as scientific research and develops his research abilities through stamp-collecting. In terms of his research, Cheng ikes to collect bird stamps most. Many of his relatives and students abroad often send him bird stamps as a gift. In this way he has amassed a lot of bird stamps from many countries.

Unfortunately, most of his precious and rare stamps were burned during the Cultural Revolution. Not only were his stamps damaged, but also his scientific certificates, photographs, doctorial gown and hat, even his suits and ties were destroyed by the Red Guards. So now you would not be able to find his graduate or wedding photographs. The only remaining cultural relic after the Cultural Revolution is the pair of tennis rackets. They survived because the Red Guards did not know what they were. However, Cheng's particular views about stamp-collecting couldn't be damaged as it is beneficial to bird research. Among the 24 sub-species of birds discovered in China after the foundation of the new China, the 16 of them are associated with Cheng. From this, you could probably find some relationship between stamp-collecting and bird-loving.

* * * * * *

Fuzhou, capital of Fujian province, is Cheng Tso-hsin's home town. He has not returned since he left there in 1948, which he regrets. In the 1950s he went to many provinces to study birds. However, he did not go to Fujian because he thought the avifauna there was relatively clear. Afterwards, although there were some opportunities for him to return, either lack of time or his health prevented him. But how much he misses his native land is often reflected in his words or his writings. He misses his relatives, colleagues and students still.

Every achievement in his work reminds him of his hometown, because he thinks it is the elders and teachers there who helped him lay a solid base. When encountering difficulties in his work, he recalls his home-land and the high expectations of him from the people there to encourage him to overcome his difficulties. On his birthday every year, Cheng's relatives in Fujian often send him some special local products such as xianmian (a kind of noodle), yanpi (a speciality of Fuzhou) and fengan (another speciality of Fuzhou) which he likes to eat very much. Even during the Cultural Revolution when he was shut in the cowshed, they didn't stop sending him gifts. He often thinks that he has received so much from his home town, but contributed too little to her.

In 1991, Cheng sent his prize-winning books with his signature in them to the hunter, Tang Ruigan, who was his assistant when he worked in Fujian, to express his gratitude. Tang Ruigan helped Cheng to collect numerous bird specimens 50 years ago.

Cheng pays close attention to the construction of the Wuyishan Nature Reserve in Fujian province. He reads every issue of *Wuyi Science* carefully, underlining important points and passes them on to colleagues. He cares for his old colleagues and students who are still working in Fujian as scientific reasearchers or teachers, and he keeps in close touch with them. Of course he was concerned with the construction and development of Fujian after China started the reform and open policy.

In 1992, Fujian Normal University celebrated her 75th anniversary and Cheng Tso-hsin took a long walk with difficulty to the post office to send a congratulatory telegram (in the 1950s Fujian Christian University became Fujian Normal University). The walk was very dangerous for him because of his illness, weak eyesight and the heavy traffic. His family scolded him for what he had done. But he said he had to send the telegraph himself to convey his affection. Although Cheng himself couldn't go back to Fujian, his wife, children and grandsons have been back many times. They always describe the changes in detail to him when they return to Beijing.

He often meets colleagues and relatives in Beijing who come from Fujian. In April 1993, a delegation from Fujian Normal University led by Chen Yiqin, the president, and Hu Shaojiao, the deputy secretary, came to see him. Hosts and guests talked to each other to their hearts' content and Cheng expressed the wish

228

from the bottom of his heart that his mother-school would flourish more and more. In recent years the government of Fujian province established Fujian Provincial Guild Hall in Beijing Meetings and festivals are usually held there and Cheng was always invited to attend.

In February 1993, Lin Yijie and Yang Aijin, the first and second leader of Changle county of Fujian province, came to Beijing and invited Cheng to attend the activities in the Spring Festival. It was very cold. Because of his health, he followed his doctor's advice and stayed at home. But he asked his wife and sons to take part in the activities on his behalf. Some special local products were given to him. Cheng applauds the high-quality jasmine tea of Changle county. He seldom drinks it himself but instead keeps it carefully for honoured guests.

His leaders wanted to publish a collection of his works. He thought it over and over and then entrusted Fujian Science & Technology Press to do this work. Over the past years, a number of journalists and writers have interviewed him and written more than 100 articles about him. Among them, the reporters from Fujian province touched his heart most. He hopes the newspapers and periodicals of his hometown will express his affection for his native land.

In 1982 Wang Jinshi, a special correspondent of a magazine called *Fujian Workers,* interviewed Cheng. In his article *Birds Fly Freely in the High Sky*, he wrote that, "When he (Cheng Tso-hsin) saw the special correspondant of *Fujian Workers*, it seemed as if he shared the emotion of his recollections, pain and the pleasure as he remembered his past."

Over the years it has been very inspiring for Cheng to know that the officials of Fujian province are attaching more significance to science and technology. He believes that the economic growth of Fujian province will be rapid, the people there will soon be rich and the dreams that all people will live happily will quickly come true.

* * * * * *

On the afternoon of 17 November 1991, the Beijing alumni of Fujian Christian University (which merged into Fujian Normal University after 1949) held a reception at the Chinese Academy of Agriculture to celebrate the 75th anniversary and to congratulate

Cheng Tso-hsin's on his 85th birthday. The reception was full of deep affection for their mother school and respect for Cheng. The Alumni Association gave him a gift, a big lacquer tray, 'Golden Deer's Blessing', with the alumni's names on it, to congratulate him on his birthday. Then they read the congratulatory words to him and some alumni showed their respects to Cheng with poetry.

Most of the alumni in Beijing were Cheng's students and most of them were retired. The older alumni in their 60s and 70s gathered together and recalled the past happily. They had all achieved much in their fields. They were grateful to their mother school and Cheng for his help and teaching. Cheng hadn't thought that he could gain the reward now in Beijing for his work in Fujian in the past. He often thought what he had done was inadequate and he owed the students a debt of gratitude. He thought he ought to say more congratulatory words in the circumstances, but he only made a statement saying that he would work harder in future.

Two years later the Beijing Branch of Fujian Christian University Alumni Association celebrated the 80th birthday of Chen Jia-jian in the Chinese

231

Lydia Cheng at her 80th birthday party.

Academy of Agriculture. Cheng felt that the time
passed too quickly. They had so much to say to their
colleagues and students that they couldn't finish.
There are so many things in the past worth recalling.
The alumni association presented gifts to Chen Jia-
jian. She believed that it must be fate that gave her
such a close association with Fujian Christian
University. She studied and worked in the University
where she met Cheng and married him. Then their
marriage strengthened her contact with the University.
The period when she was in Fujian Christian
University was the most precious period of her youth.

PERFECT COMPANIONS FOR A GOLDEN MARRIAGE

On 6 January 1935, by the Chinese lunar calendar, Cheng Tso-hsin and Chen Jia-jian were married and the couple lived with each other for 50 years. They experienced together all the ups and downs, the failures and successes, the torture of difficulties and the happiness of achievements. The inflexible pursuit of a career and the unchangeable loyalty of love are the foundations of their golden marriage.

After their marriage Jia-jian did her best to help Cheng in his research in addition to her own work and housework. At Fujian Christian University she accompanied him to study in his office at night, helping him catch frogs for experiments, draw diagrams of the animals for him, and playing tennis with him as well. After having children, she did everything to help Cheng work with great concentration: she looked after his parents and old grandmother, arranged and supported the studies of his brothers, sisters and cousins, and entertained guests and students at home.

For many years, she managed the housework without any complaints. After the Anti-Japanese War

233

broke out and the University moved inland to Shaowu, the family left their home with only some clothes and food and just locked the door, thinking they would be back after several months. But it was several years before they returned, only to find that their house was empty. So the couple had to rebuild their home.

At that time Cheng's salary was not enough to support a big family, so Jia-jian had to teach in a primary school. Meanwhile she encouraged the young and old of the whole family to plant vegetables and to raise pigs and chickens to help feed them all. In 1950, Jia-jian left Nanjing for Beijing. Cheng greeted her at Beijing railway station and, reunited after a long period of separation, the couple were very excited. At the exit, because the luggage was overweight, they had to pay extra. But after they had collected every penny, they still couldn't afford it, but then Cheng remembered the notice of a contribution fee from the press in his pocket. He hurried to the accounts department of the Commercial Press of China to draw the money and then returned to the station to fetch the luggage and return home with Jia-jian.

At that time, they were assigned to live in an old temple in the city. The temple was divided into rooms so that several families could share it. Most of their furniture was brought from a second hand market. That old dining table is still at home, and has almost become an historical relic. Although life was hard then, the family was happy because the members were considerate. Before long, Jia-jian began to work in the National Women's Union. Though it was a barter system, life improved.

In 1951 The Academy of Sciences of China assigned Cheng three rooms at Shibanfang lane, West City District, so their housing improved. As the room was so small and seemed too crowded, Cheng did all his work in his office. After supper, he would walk for 20 minutes to his office and work for several hours. In 1955 the Academy of Sciences built the Institute of Zoology and the Institute of Mathematics as well as a lot of living quarters. Cheng was assigned a new apartment of five rooms and his salary was raised, so their standard of living improved and they bought new clothes and furniture. Though conditions were better, he worked on in the office as it had became his habit.

From the 1950s to the early 1960s, Cheng often went out on field trips, leaving for mountain forests like a migratory bird from spring to autumn. Certainly Cheng had no time to consider family matters. Fortunately he had a perfect wife to do all that for him. With a sorry smile, Cheng would say, "there is your sweat in my achievement at work."

During the Cultural Revolution, Cheng was locked up in a cattle shed with only 33 yuan a month to live on. His elder son was also separated for investigation, receiving little more than 20 yuan a month. Jia-jian cut expenses and used the savings of previous years, since the two children were in university and three little grandsons needed servants to look after them.

The financial difficulties could be overcome, but not the worry. Jia-jian was worried that Cheng would suffer physical torture for being frank and outspoken and that he wouldn't be able to tolerate the merciless criticism, since he was more than 60 and had high blood pressure. The strain everyday gradually made Jia-jian neurasthenic and she couldn't sleep well. One day, when someone from the Institute brought Cheng's salary, she hurriedly wrote a few words on a note to Cheng saying "believe in the people; believe in the country."

Before long, the family was allowed to take medicine to him. She mixed beef and chicken soup with cypress soup which could reduce blood pressure to guarantee nutrition for Cheng's health (perhaps this is her own invention). After six months Cheng was allowed to return home. The couple were reunited and too excited to know what to say. Jia-jian said continually "it's wonderful to have you home."

In August 1966, the Red Guards searched Cheng's house and confiscated his possessions. They even made him put on a doctor's gown and cap and made him stand on the balcony to be exposed publicly. The piano, sofa, TV, wardrobe, quilts and clothes, were loaded onto a ten-wheeled lorry and taken away. What hurt Cheng most was that his new typewriter, which he had just bought, was taken away. Jia-jian told him "the first thing we will buy is a new typewriter as soon as we have the money". His wife's understanding was the greatest comfort to him.

From 1971, after she retired, Jia-jian plunged into helping Cheng's research work. She drew pictures, researched place names, typed and edited his reports and indexes. The leaders of the Institute all praised Cheng for his perfect wife. With her help, Cheng's several works, such as *Avifauna of the Qinling Range* (1973), *Fauna Sinica--Aves. Vol.4. Galliformes* (1978), *Fauna Sinica--Aves . Vol.2. Anseriformes* (1979), and *Birds of Xizang (Tibet)* (1982) were published.

From 1987, Cheng was hospitalised twice for long periods due to heart problems. Jia-jian waited on for him day and night. She herself was already more than 70, with coronary problems too. But she nursed Cheng patiently and carefully despite her own illness. Jia-jian stayed with Cheng in the hospital day and night all by herself so that the children's work would not suffer from having to nurse their father. One year she accompanied Cheng to hospital for eight months, but when he was well, she had to be hospitalised herself. In Beijing Hospital people respectfully looked at the grey-haired old couple as they walked the passage, arm in arm, praising their obvious affection for each other.

After she retired from the National Women's Union, apart from doing the housework, Jia-jian subscribed to many newspapers and magazines to acquaint herself with important domestic and overseas affairs and the policies of the party. Wanting to make the most of her remaining years as an old comrade, she did voluntary work as an advisor for several kindergartens which were attached to the Zhongguan Village Administration Bureau of the Academy of Sciences. People honoured her with the title 'Master Chen'. She gave lectures to the kindergarten teachers, prepared lessons with them, listened to their courses and led them on visits to advanced kindergartens to improve the professional level of the teachers.

She also worked for the neighbourhood committee continuously, busy from upstairs to downstairs with those miscellaneous and trivial affairs. In 1984, she was elected as a member of the Zhongguancun Village Neighbourhood Committee and took part in the sixth and seventh Women Representives Meeting of Haidian district. In 1985, she was elected advanced individual for old people's work in Haidian district and in November was commended by the Beijing municipality. And she was once honoured with 'the little retired but not resting comrade' by the National Woman's Union and the Communist Youth League central committee.

In May 1986, she organized her family to take part in the 'family joy' singing contest of Beijing municipality. Every Sunday she, her children and her grandchildren practiced singing together. Cheng expressed his support and voluntarily acted as a conductor. The concientiousness of the old couple impressed their juniors. Obediently they took part in the practices. More than ten members of Cheng's family took part in the performance and they earned first prize in Haidian district and were qualified for the Beijing municipal contest. On the day however, Jia-jian was in hospital and although advised not to take part she insisted on going. In the morning, the doctor gave her a injection to bring her fever down. In the afternoon she was driven by a comrade of the culture centre to the theatre. Their performance won the Beijing municipal prize and a video recording was broadcast several times on TV. A reporter photographed Cheng when he was conducting the family's singing which was printed in the English edition of the *People's Pictorial.*

In March 1988 Jia-jian attended the Beijing municipal meeting which cited the March 8 models and the "Five-good family" models. She also attended the Beijing municipal family education workshop, discussing family education with others. Because of

Enjoying a family chorus.

241

her experience she had the authority to express opinions. Early in the 1950, she had already applied to join the Chinese Communist Party and she was admitted as a member in 1987 when she was 75. In 1991, she was elected committee member in charge of propaganda of her party branch. She was honoured with the title Excellent Party Member in 1991 and 1992.

Since they had spent 54 happy years together and had achieved a lot in their careers, they were elected 'perfect companions for golden marriage' in a national competition in 1989. At the ceremony on 8 October 1989 Jia-jian, representing the 103 couples who had won made a thank-you speech which the TV news reported on the same day and their achievement was made into a television film named *The Love of Half a Century* by CCTV which was broadcast several times on TV. They received congratulatory letters from relatives and friends everywhere.

On 10 March 1990 the *Beijing Daily* published an article to introduce the film *The Love of Half A Century* which read "In the pictures of this film, a crane embroidered on the tie of the famous biologist Cheng Tso-hsin, is emphasized several times. With the development of the story, people begin to realize the special empathy which the couple, Cheng Tso-hsin and Jia-jian Chen, have for cranes. In the family of flying birds, mandarin ducks are always together but with a pair of cranes if one dies, the other dies as a consequence. Cheng Tso-hsin wears a tie on which his wife had embroidered a crane and there is much significance in this. In married life, the most moving scene is not the love which makes them drunk and infatuated at first but the reliance and understanding between a couple when they are old. They sit together. Without saying a word everything is understood."

Professor and Mrs Cheng selected as one of 103 couples in China to be given the honour of participating in the Golden Wedding celebrations.

Their golden wedding celebrations lasted until March 1992. Beijing Purple House Wedding Centre held a golden wedding ceremony for the perfect companions who lived in Beijing. They presented gifts to each other. Cheng gave Jia-jian a golden key, which he had preserved for scores of years. In return, Jia-jian presented him with a golden pen, which was a 'weapon' that Cheng couldn't live without for a day. The photograph, in which they were holding their hands highly to express thanks, was printed on the right hand corner of the first page of *Guangming Daily,* 8 March 1992.

Professor Cheng and Lydia Cheng with their family.

TIME WAITS FOR NOBODY

'Time waits for nobody' is the motto by which Cheng Tso-hsin lives. In his opinion, life is so limited that a person should make the best use of time to do more work. He lives a regular life with a full work schedule. That his daily life is based on his study of biological science is generally acknowledged by those around him. He always goes to bed early and gets up early. He pays attention to what he eats and drinks, is never fastidious about his meals and he eats everything as long as he thinks it good for his health. Cheng eats heartily at festivals, but never eats or drinks too much at one meal. He lives 'scientifically' without bad habits such as smoking and drinking, which ensures his good health. He has walked across almost every mountain and river in China and even after he retired, he continued to undertake vital scientific research. A healthy body is the basis for him to implement the motto.

He established the habit of getting up early every morning to observe birds when he was a young man. He would get up at five o'clock, make breakfast and then go to the gate of the Institute of Zoology. The

The basket of flowers presented by the China Ornithological Society celebrating Prof Cheng's 88th birthday. Beijing, 18 November 1994.

guard always opened the gate for him ahead of time and he was the first arrival at the Institute for years until he was 80 years old. From then on, his doctor did not allow him to go to his office because of his heart disease and so he began to work at home after that.

Cheng laid stress on a proper balance between work and rest, although he did not keep up this habit when he became old. He felt that time was so limited and he wanted to make up for time lost, especially the ten years of the Cultural Revolution.

In order to leave some contribution to the country and to future generations, he worked hard to bring about his plans one by one. "Making unremitting

246

efforts to improve myself and to work for the future of my motherland" was his contribution to the book *The famous remarks of contemporary Chinese scientists.* His deeds have matched his words. There is nothing in his mind except for work. He works everyday come wind, rain or snow, cold or heat. He works the whole day in his office; the leaders knew that Cheng would even work on New Years Day, so they would tell the guards not to close his office on holidays. He ate in the laboratory and slept in the office when he was busy. He did not change this habit until he was in his seventieth year. The only difference was he often took a pot which contained medicine.

Once heavy rain made it difficult to walk in the streets, but Cheng insisted on going to his office. Nobody could persuade him not to go. Half way, a strange driver asked him to get in and kindly took him to his office. Doctors gave him a certificate for sick leave because of his high blood pressure and heart disease, but he never used it. He could not part with his work. He often said "time waits for nobody". He once worked for such a long time in spite of his illness that he fainted on the stairs of the Zoology Institute in December, 1990. He was given emergency treatment at Beijing Hospital. When he came to, his colleagues advised him to balance work and rest properly. But he said "As soon as I think that I am old I do not have much time. I can't helping using all my time in my work." His doctor demanded he stay in the hospital. After he had been examined he asked the doctor "Can I go to work? I will only accept the cure which can make me work again. If I can't work any more, I do not need to live a longer life."

He can't live without work, so he changed his ward into a work room with books, materials and a typewriter. He often wrote, corrected proofs, answered letters, met visitors and reporters. He even called his colleagues and graduate students to his ward to discuss experiments, all of which made his health worse. Thereafter his doctors prevented him from doing anything except lying in bed and demands which were not good for his health were refused. He asked the doctors to allow him to listen to the radio, which he was permitted because music might help his recuperation.

One day the doctor heard strange voices coming out from his ward, " der-da, der-da..." It was neither music nor news but was a voice pronouncing a foreign language. The doctor was amazed at Cheng's intelligence. He had mastered English and already knew German, French and Russian, but he was still working hard at learning another new language. The doctor withdrew without forbidding him.

Cheng used his entire eight months in the hospital to amend *Economic Birds of China*, to edit *Fauna Sinica--Aves Vol. 10 Passeriformes: Muscicapidae I Turdinae* and to draw up a conclusion for a PhD. After he was discharged from hospital he said he would never return there again. This was not the hospital's fault; in fact the conditions of the Beijing Hospital were perfect but he wanted to make the best use of

Professor Cheng at work.

Professor Cheng awarded with a 'Lifelong Honorary Award in Wildlife Conservation' in December 1993.

time and get rid of the hospital restrictions in order to finish his annual writing targets. Since the foundation of the People's Republic of China, the leaders asked him many times to recuperate at Mount Lushan, Qing Dan, and Hainan Island. But he only once went to Beidaihe. Because of his busy schedule, he gave up the other opportunities. He had investigated the whole county but had no time for the beautful lake in Hang zhou and wonderland in Guilin.

He disliked family chatter to kill time and he always fussed if his daughter and son came home and wanted to have a chat with mother about family life.

That he always urged the family to do something useful seems not unreasonable. Because Cheng has always made the best use of time, he has managed to do a lot of field work gathering and sorting out material and he finished 16 monographs, about 30 books, 130 treatises and 250 popular science books all amounting to 10 million characters. What energy he has! Someone asked "Prof Cheng, what's your maxim?" He answered "Life is limited, but knowledge is boundless; we must not waste any time." Another question was "What is your ambition?" He answered "As a Chinese, I want to leave something behind and to contribute my bit to my nation".

Professor Cheng with his doctorate and post-doctorate students in the Institute of Zoology, CAS in September 1994.

THE CHRONICLE OF PROF CHENG TSO-HSIN

18 November 1906 Born in Fuzhou City, Fujian province.

1912-1918   Studied in the Cang Xia Zhou Primary School in Fuzhou.

1918-1922   Studied in the High School attached to the Youth Association in Fuzhou.

1922-1926   Studied in department of Biology, Fujian Christian University. Graduated with Bachelor degree.

1926-1930   Studied in the Graduate School of the University of Michigan, USA. Graduated with MSc, ScD and the Sigma XI Key.

1930-1947   Director and Professor of the Department of Biology, Fujian Christian University. 1933 Edited *The Laboratory Manual of General Biology in Universities* (the first textbook of biology to be written in Chinese).

1934   One of the founders of the China Zoological Society.

1936-1940   Concurrently Director of Biological Department, Fujian Scientific Musium.

1938   Edited the textbook of *General Biology* for University students.

1938-1947   Dean of Studies, Fujian Christian University.

1944   Published *A Three-Year Census of the Birds of Shaowu.*

1945-1946   Invited to the United States of America and held Visiting Professorship under sponsorship of the

Cultural Relationship Bureau of the State
Department.

1946-1947 Returned to Fujian Christian University as
Professor, Dean of Studies and Dean of the
Science College. Published *Checklist of Chinese
Birds*. (the first Checklist of Chinese birds written
by a Chinese.)

1947-1949 Senior editor of the Natural Science Department,
National Centre of Compilation and Translation;
Part-time Professor of the Central University.

1950-1956 Curator and secretary of the Specimen Curative
Committee, Academia Sinica. Senior editor and
director of the scientific terms office of the Bureao
of Compilation and Translation, Academia Sinica.

1951-present Joined the Jiu-San Learned Society as member of
the central Council; now committee member of
the Central Canyi Commission.

1952 Published *The taxonomy of the vertebrates*.

1953-present Research fellow of Institute of Zoology, Academia
Sinica; Director of the Ornithological Department,
Animal Resource Department, Department of
Vertebrate Systematics and Faunastics. Editor-in-
chief of Acta Zoological Sinica, Acta
Zootaxonomic Sinica, Sinozoology, Chinese
Journal of Zoology. Took charge of the founding
of the bird-specimen room of Institute of Zoology.

1954-1961 Concurrently Professor of biological departments
of Peking University, Beijing Normal University,
Northwest University, Lanzhou University and
Shandong University.

253

1955-1958	Edited *Distributional list of Chinese birds: Non-passeriformes and passeriformes.*
1956	Secretary in General of China Zoological Society.
1957	Published *Studies of insect-eating birds in Chang-li orchard district of Hebei province.* (with Qian Yan-Wen).
1958-1959	Visited Eastern Germany and Soviet Union.
1960	Published *The dividing of zoological regions in China* (with Zhang Rong-Zu.) Corresponding member of German Ornithological Society and Japan Ornithological Society. Edited *The ten years' achievements of Chinese Zoology* and *The ten years' achievements of Chinese Zoogeography.*
1962	Editor-in-chief of *Economic birds in China.* (Subsequently translated into English by the US Department of Commission.) Member and vice director of the editorial board of *Fauna Sinica.*
1964	Edited *Systematic keys to the Chinese birds.*
1966	Edited *Systematic keys to the Chinese birds* (revised edition).
1973	Edited *Avifauna of Qin-ling Range*, with Qian Yan-Wen and Li Gui-Yuan.
1976	Advisor to the International Crane Foundation, USA.
1978	Editor-in-chief of *Fauna Sinica-Aves. vol. 4: Galliformes.* Editor-in-chief of the Zoological and Zoogeographical Sections of *Chinese Encyclopedia.* Published *Distribution list of Chinese birds* (second edition). Won a personal prize (*Systematic studies on the birds in China*); a

prize for two persons (*The dividing of zoological regions in China*) and a collective prize (*Fauna Sinica*) on the National Scientific Meeting. Vice president of the China Zoological Society. Visited Britain and attended the International Symposium of the World Pheasant Association (WPA). Vice president of WPA and corresponding member of the British Ornithologists' Union.

1979   Editor-in-chief of *Fauna Sinica-Aves. vol. 2: Anseriformes.*

1980   In January led a Chinese delegation to Hokkaido, Japan and attended the International Symposium of Waterfowl and Cranes. In April joined the delegation of Academia Sinica to visit America, and held negotiations for co-operation. Elected as an academician of Academia Sinica. Member of the China National Federation for Science and Technical member of the compiling committee of the National Atlas. Took charge of Zoology in the International Symposium of the Investigation of Qinghai-Tibetan Plateau. In October, led Chinese museological delegation to attend the anniversary conference in Australia. In November, joined the Chinese delegation to Japan to hold negotiations for Sino-Japan migratory bird protection. Sponsor of the China Ornithological Society and the first president of the Society. Corresponding member of the American Ornithologists' Union.

1981   Deputy director of Beijing Natural History Museum and Director of the Natural History

Institute. In October, *Distributional list of Chinese birds* won an honorary award of the University of Michigan.

1982   Published *Vertebrate Taxonomy* and won the gold prize of the National Scientific and Technical Publications. *Fauna Sinica- Aves. vol. 2: Anseriformes.* won the second class prize of the Scientific Progress, Chinese Academy of Sciences.

1983   Research tutor of the doctorate students. Editor-in-chief of *Birds of Xizang (Tibet)*. Vice president of the Chinese Wililife Conservation Association.

1984   President of China Zoological Society. Honorary member of the American Ornithologists' Union. Invited by Hong Kong Natural Conservation Association for a visit to Hong Kong on academic exchanges.

1985   Member of China National Committee on Scientific Terms, and advisor to the committee on Chinese Scientific Terms of Zoology.

1986   Honorary president of China Ornithological Society. President of the World Pheasant Association.

1987   Editor-in-chief on *Fauna Sinica-Aves. vol.11: Passeriformes: Muscicapidea II. Timaliinae* and won second class prize of natural science Chinese Academy of Sciences. Published *A Synopsis of the Avifauna of China* (in English). Attended the First International Wildlife Conservation Conference acting as chairman of the Chinese delegation.

1988   Won the Special Conservation Achievement

Award of National Wildlife Federation, U.S.A.

1989   *Synopsis of the avifauna of China* given the first-
class award in natural sciences by the Chinese
Academy of Sciences, the second-class award by
the National Commission of Sciences and
Technology, a special award by the National
Association of Publications, and an honorary
medal by the academic committee of Academia
Sinica. In October, attended the fourth
International Symposium of World Pheasant
Association, and made plenary report of the
studies on pheasants in China. Elected as honorary
president of the China Zoological Society.

1991   Editor-in-chief of *Fauna Sinica-Aves. vol.6:
Columbiformes-Strigiformes.* Donated all awards
of *A Synopsis of the Avifauna of China* to the
China Ornithological Society to set up a
foundation for The Cheng Tso-Hsin Award for
Young Ornithologists.

1993   Editor-in-chief of *Economic birds of China*
(second edition) and *Fauna Sinica-Aves. vol. 10:
Passeriformes: Muscicapidea I. Turdinae.*
Compiled *A complete checklist of species and
subspecies of the Chinese birds* (in English).

1993   Presented with a Lifelong Honorary Award in
wildlife conservation by China Wildlife
Conservation Association at the conference
celebrating the tenth anniversary of its founding.

1994   Elected honorary president of the XXII
International Ornithological Congress.

SELECTED ORNITHOLOGICAL PUBLICATIONS

of

Prof Cheng Tso-Hsin (Zheng Zuo-Xin)

(not including textbooks, technical brochures, encyclopedia entries, and more than 250 popular articles) - December 1994, Beijing, China.

I   Ornithological monographs and handbooks

1.   Distributional list of Chinese birds. vol. 1 (non-passeriformes): 1-328. Science Press (1955).

2.   Studies of insect-eating birds in Chang-Li orchard district of Hebei province. 1-137. Science Press (1957)

3.   Distribution list of Chinese birds. vol. 2 (passeriformes): 1-591. Science Press (1957)

4.   The dividing of zoological regions in China.1-66. Science Press (1958).

5.   Economic birds of China, 1963, 1-896; 2nd ed., 1994, 1-619. Science Press.

6.   Systematic keys to Chinese birds with distributional checklist.1-374. Science Press.(1964)

7.   Systematic keys to the Chinese birds (revised edition).1-251. Science Press (1966)

8.   Avifauna of the Qin-ling Range. 1-140. Science Press (1973).

9.   Distribution list of Chinese birds. (second edition).1-1218. Science Press (1976).

10.   Fauna Sinica-Aves.vol.4. Galliformes.1-200. Science Press (1978).

11.   Fauna Sinica-Aves.vol.2. Anseriformes 1-144. Science Press (1979).

12.   Birds of Xizang (Tibet). 1-353. Science Press (1983).

13.   Fauna Sinica-Aves. vol.11. Passeriformes: Muscicapidae II. Timaliinae: 1-305. Science Press (1987).

14.   A synopsis of the avifauna of China .1-1224. Science Press and Paul Parey Scientific Publishers (1987).

15.   Fauna Sinica-Aves. vol.6: Columbiformes-Strigiformes. Science Press (1991).

16.   Selected ornithological papers of Cheng Tso-Hsin. 1-413. Fujian Science and Technological Press (1993).

17.   A complete checklist of species and subspecies of the Chinese birds. 1-318. Science Press (1994).

18.   Fauna Sinica-Aves. vol. 10. Passeriformes: Muscicapidae I. Turdinae: 1-239. Science Press (1995).

II.   Ornithological papers

1.   A list of Chinese birds heretofore recorded only from Fukien province. China Journ. 20(3): 150-158 (1934).

2.   A check-list of birds heretofore recorded from Fukien province. Fukien Chr. Univ.Sci.Journ.1:1-58(1938).

3.   A preliminary check- list of birds heretofore recorded from Kwangtung and nearby islands including Hainan. Part 1. Non-passerine birds. Lingnan Sci. Journ.19(2):133-181(1949).

4. Studies of birds of the Min-jiang Valley, Fujian Province. I. Non-Passeriformes. Biol. Bull. 2:1-72(1940).

5. Notes on bird observations during the summer along the Shaowu Stream. Peking Nat. Hist. Bull. 15(3):235-241(1941).

6. A winter census of birds along the Shaowu Stream in North Fukien. Peking Nat. Hist. Bull. 16(1):85-90 (1941).

7. A green pigeon, *Sphenurus sieboldii sieboldii* (Temminck) from Shaowu, Fukien . China Journ. 25(2):71-73(1941).

8. Birds of the Gu-ling Mountain (Fuzhou City) during the summer. Science 25(7-8):450-459 (1941).

9. Studies of birds of the Min-jiang Valley, Fujian Province. II. Passeriformes (Alaudidae--Sylviidae). Biol. Bull. 3:1-50 (1942).

10. Census of birds of Shaowu District for three years (1938-41).Biol. Bull. 4:63-150 (1944).

11. Birds of Wu-yi mountains. Biol. Bull 4:163-170(1944).

12. Studies of birds of Min-jiang valley. III. Passeriformes (Muscacipodae-Fringillidae). Biol. Bull. 5:3-50(1947).

13. Birds collected from Shun-chang and Jiang-Io districts. Biol. Bull. 5:132-136(1947).

14. Statistical studies of the birds of China . Science 30:141(1947).

15. A preliminary study of the geographical distribution of birds in China. Science 30:139(1947).

16. Checklist of Chinese birds. Trans. Chin. Assoc. Adv. Sci. 9: 49-84 (1947).

17. Notes on the avifauna of Shaowu, Fukien. Lingnan Sci. Journ. 22: 105-114 (1948).

260

18. A preliminary check-list of birds heretofore recorded from Kwangtung and nearby islands including Hainan. Part II. Passeriform birds. Peking Nat. Hist. Bull. 17:23-68(1948).

19. Geographical distribution of the Chinese birds. 13th Congr. Inter. Zool., Paris, 1948 (1949), 408-410.

20. On the geographical distribution of birds in China. Peking Nat. Hist Bull. 18:45-57(1949).

21. A Study of the geographical distribution of birds in China. Chin. Journ. Zool. 4: 97-108 (1949).

22. A preliminary census of locust-eating birds found in the Wei-shan lake area and vicinity. Acta Agric. Sinica 6(2):145-155(1955).

23. On a tentative scheme for dividing zoogeographical regions of China. Acta Geog. Sinica. 22(1):93-109(1956).

24. A new form of the white-backed woodpecker (*Dendrocopos Leucotos tangi* subsp. nov.) from Szechwan, China. Acta Zool. Sinica 8(2): 133-142. (1956).

25. New records of Chinese birds from southern Yunnan. Acta Zool. Sinica. 9(1):34-45. (1957).

26. Food analysis of the Tree-Sparrow (Passer montanus saturatus). Acta Zool. Sinica 9(3):255-266(1957).

27. On the wintering ecology of the Rook in the suburbs of Beijing. Chin. Journ. Zool. 1(4):1-5(1957).

28. New records of Chinese birds from southern Yunnan , China. II. Non-Passerine birds from the Hsi-Shuan-Pan-Na area in southern Yunnan. Acta Zool. Sinica 10(1):83-92(1958).

261

29. New records of Chinese birds from southern Yunnan, China. III. Passerine birds from Hsi-Shuan-Pan-Na area in southern Yunnan. Acta Zool. Sinica 10(1):93-102(1958).
30. Nests and eggs of the breeding birds in the Summer Palace, Beijing. Chin. Journ. Zool. 2(2):74-82(1958).
31. Systematic Keys to the species of *Anatidae* in China. Chin. Journ. Zool. 3(3):103-104(1959).
32. The pheasants of China and their distribution. Serial Publ. Zool. 1:68-78.
33. Studies on the breeding behaviour of some insect-eating birds in the fruit-producing district of Chang-li, Hebei province. I. Parus major artatus Thayer et Bangs. Acta Zool. Sinica II(1) : 101-115 (1959).
34. Studies on the breeding behaviour of some insect-eating birds in the fruit-producing district of Chang-li, Hebei province. II. Acta Zool. Sinica 12(1):139-148(1960).
35. Discovery of *Branta ruficollis* in China. Chin. Journ. Zool. 4(6): 256(1960).
36. Birds of Huang-Shan mt. in Anhuei province. Chin. Journ. Zool. 4(1):10-14) (1960).
37. Studies on birds from southern Yunnan II. Acta Zool. Sinica 12(2): 250-277(1960).
38. A preliminary survey of Hunan province. Part I. non-Passeriformes. Acta Zool. Sinica 12(2):293-319(1960).
39. A preliminary survey of birds of Hunan province. Part I. non-Passeriformes. Acta Zool. Sinica 13(1-4):97-121 (1961).
40. On birds from the Hsi-Shuan-Pan-Na area and Yunnan province. I. Acta Zool. Sinica 13(1-4):53-69 (1961).

41. Ein ubersehener Brutvogel der Palearktis: "Emberiza siamsseni" Martens. Journ. f. Orn. 102:152-153(1961).

42. On birds from the Hsi-Shuan-Pan-Na area and vicinity in Yunnan province. III. Acta Zool. Sinica 14(1): 74-94 (1962).

43. A systematic review of *pomatorhinus* heretofore recorded from China. Acta Zool. Sinca 14(2): 197-218 (1962).

44. Two new records of Chinese birds from southern Yunnan: *Garrulax ruficollis* and *Ptyonoprogne concolor*. Acta Zool. Sinica 14(2): 287 (1962)

45. Survey of avian and mammalian resources in western Sichuan and northern Yunnan. Special publication by Academia Sinica 89-122, Appendix:1-20 (1962)

46. An avifaunal survey of the Tsinling and Ta-Pa-Shan Region. Acta Zool. Sinica 14(3):361-380(1962).

47. A new generic record to the Chinese Avifauna: *Oxyura leucocephala* (Scopoli). Acta Zool. Sinica 14(3):431(1962).

48. Taxonomic studies on birds from southwestern Szechwan and northwestern Yunnan. Part I. non-Passeriformes. Acta Zool. Sinica 14(4):537-554(1962).

49. Taxonomic studies on birds from southwestern Szechwan and northwestern Yunnan. Part II. Passeriformes: *Muscicapidae*. Acta Zool. Sinica 15(1):109-124(1963).

50. Taxonomic studies on birds from southwestern Szechwan and northwestern Yunnan. Part III. Passeriformes (cont'd). Acta Zool. Sinica 15(2):295-316(1963).

51. Studies on birds of Mount Omei (Szechwan) and their vertical distribution. Acta Zool. Sinica 15(2):317-335(1963).

52. A new generic record to the Chinese avifauna: Callene Blyth (*Muscicapidae: Turdinae*). Acta Zool.Sinica 15(2):339 (1963).

53. Sub-specific differentiation of the two sibling species of the necklaced laughing thrushes(*Garrulax pectoralis* and *G. moniligerus*) in China, including a new sub-species: *Garrulax pectoralis pingi.* Acta Zool. Sinica 15(3):471-478(1963).

54. Subspecific differentation of the Red-Winged Shrike-Babbler (*Pteruthius flaviscapis*) in China, including a new subspecies: *P.f. lingshuiensnsis.* Acta Zool. Sinica 15(4):639-647(1963).

55. Preliminary studies on the breeding behaviour of the tree-sparrow (*Passer montanus saturatus*). Acta Zool. Sinica 15(4):527-536(1963).

56. A new subspecies of sapphire-headed flycatcher from Szechwan, China: *Ficedula sapphira tienchuanensis (Muscicapidae:Muscicapinae).* Acta Zool.Sinica 16(1):161-164(1964).

57. On the vertical distribution of birds on mount Yu-Lung, NW Yunnan. Acta Zool. Sinica 16(2):295-314(1964).

58. A new subspecies of the velvet-fronted nuthatch from Hainan : *Sitta frontalis chienfangensis,* subsp. nov. Acta Zootaxonomica Sinica 1(1): 1-5 (1964).

59. New records to the Chinese avifauna, including those of a family (*Podargidae*) and two genera. Acta Zool. Sinica 16(3): 487-493(1964).

60. A new subspecies of the silver pheasant from Szechwan, China: *Lophura nycthemera omeiensis.* Acta Zootaxonomica Sinica 1(2): 221-228 (1964).

264

61. An avifauna survey of the Ching-Hai province. Acta Zool. Sinica 16(4): 690-709 (1964).

62. Avifaunal studies of the Yun-Shuh Autonomous Region, Chinghai province. Acta Zool. Sinica 17(2): 217-229 (1965).

63. On the validity of the genus *Pseudopodoces*. Acta Zootaxonomica Sinica 2(2): 178-182 (1965).

64. On the avifauna of north-western Szechwan. Acta Zool. Sinica 17(4): 435-450 (1965).

65. New records of birds from the south-western parts of China. Chin. Journ. Zool. 7(1):11-13 (1965).

66. The gorgetless form of the orange-gorgetted flycatcher (*Ficedula strophiata Hodgson*) from Szechean province. Acta Zool. Sinica 17(1):103-104 (1965)

67. Survey of birds in the Hong-Hua-Er-Ji Town of Hulun-Buir-Meng of Nei Mongol Autonomous Region. Chin. Journ. Zool. 1965(2):71-73 (1965).

68. A new three-toed parrotbill from Tsinling Range, Shensi, China. Acta Zool. Sinica 19(1):48-50(1973).

69. A new subspecies of *Treron sieboldii* from the Tsingling Range, Shensi, China. Acta Zool. Sinica 19(1):51-53 (1973).

70. New records of Chinese birds from western Yunnan. Acta Zool. Sinica 19(2):199-200 (1973)

71. New records of Chinese birds from western Yunnan. Acta Zool. Sinica 19(4):420(1973).

72. On the birds of Hainan. II. Acta Zool. Sinica 19(4):405-416(1973)

73. A new name for *Pomatorhinus ruficollis intermedius Cheng*, 1962. Acta Zool. Sinica 20(1):108 (1974).

265

74. A new subspecies of *Dendrocopos major* from the Inner Mongolian region: *D.m.wulashanicus*. Acta Zool. Sinica 21(4):385-388 (1975).

75. Taxonomic notes on *Zosterops japonica* of Hainan Island, Acta Zool. Sinica 25(2):187(1979).

76. The relationship between breeding species of birds and migration in different latitudes. Acta Zool. Sinica 25(2):188(1979).

77. A sketch of the avian fauna of China with special reference to galliforme species. Proc. Woodland Grouse Symp. (World Pheasant Association): 45-47 (1979).

78. Taxonomic and ecological notes of capercaillies and black grouse in China. Proc. Woodland Grouse Symp. (World Pheasant Association): 83-86(1979).

79. On subspecific differentiation of the silver pheasant (*Lophura nycthemera*). Journ.World Pheasant Association: 42-46(1979).

80. Great numbers of bird species found in China. Tori 28(1): 59-62(1979).

81. A new subspecies of *Tragopan caboti: Tragopan caboti guangxiensis*. Acta Zool. Sinica 25(3):292-294(1979).

82. Preliminary studies on systematic relationships of the species of Mergus. Acta Zootaxonomica Sinica 5(1):102-105(1980).

83. New records of Chinese birds from Xizang(Tibet). Acta Zool. Sinica 26(3):286-287(1980).

84. Cranes in China. Crane Research, International Crane Foundation. 47-48(1982).

85. On the land-vertebrate fauna of Qinghai-Xizang (Tibetan) Plateau with consideration concerning its history of

tranformation. Mem. Beijing Nat. Hist. Mus. 9(1): 1-21 (1981).

86. A new subspecies of *Garrulax galbanus* from Yunnan, China: *Garrulax galbanus sinaoensis*. Sinozoologia 2:1-2 (1982).

87. Preliminary studies on the avifauna of the Mount Wuyi area. Wuyi Science Journ. 1:153-167 (1981).

88. On the evolution of Garrulax (*timaliinae*), with comparative studies of the species found at the centre and those on the periphery of the distributional range of the genus. Acta Zool. Sinica 28(3): 205-210 (1982).

89. A new subspecies of *Paradoxornis zappeyi: P.z. erlangshanicus,* Acta Zootaxonomica Sinica 8(3): 328-330 (1983).

90. On the evolution of *Garrulax*, with consideration concerning characteristics of the species found at the place of origin of the genus. Selected Works on Evolution: 149-150 (1983).

91. Studies on some important insect-eating birds from western Yunnan. Zool. Res. 5(1): 57-66 (1984).

92. On the Meridiomal Himalayas as the probable place of origin of the genus *Garrulax* in China. Special Pub. Qinhai-Tibetan Plateau. I: 288-289 (1983).

93. A systematic review of c row-tits (*Paradoxornis*) hitherto recorded from China. Acta Zool. Sinica 30(3):278-285(1984).

94. The progress of zoogeographical research in China. Mem. Beijing Nat. Hist. Mus. 27:1-10(1984).

95. Systematic keys to cranes of the world. Acta Zool. Sinica 32(2): 189-193(1986)

96. The avifauna of Taiwan province, as compared with that of neighbouring regions. Wuyi Sci. Journ. 6:257-265(1986).
97. Taxonomic hos *Paradoxonis flavirostris.* Var Fagelvarld 8/88:463 (in Swedish).
98. An overview of research on pheasants in China. 1978-1988. Proc. 4th Intern. Symp. World Pheasant Association: 1-10 (1989).
99. A taxonmic revision of *Paradoxornis webbianos* (G. R. Gray). Acta Zootaxonomica Sinica 18(1):108-113(1993).
100. On the development of ornithology in ancient China. Studies Hist. Nat. Sci. 12(2):159-165(1993)
101. On the development of ornithology in recent China. Wuyi Sci. Journ. 10:90-97(1993).
102. On the history of census concering the number of species of Chinese birds. Acta Zootaxonomica Sinica 19(1):4-9(1993).
103. Wing-shortening-a distinctive feature of subspeciation of island birds. Proc. XXI Intern. Orn. Congress. (Abstract already published by the Congress; full text in press.)

MEMBERSHIP OF THE WORLD PHEASANT ASSOCIATION

Membership of the World Pheasant Association is open to all those in sympathy with WPA's aims and willing to comply with its rules. The Association is an international registered charity with members in over forty countries. It is recognised by IUCN and BirdLife International as the authoritative body for the worldwide conservation of the Galliformes (pheasants and other gamebirds).

The World Pheasant Association, PO Box 5, Lower Basildon, Reading, Berks RG8 9PF. Telephone (01734) 845140 (24 hr Answerphone) Facsimile: (01734) 843369

Aims of the Association

**WPA AIMS TO DEVELOP AND PROMOTE
THE CONSERVATION OF ALL SPECIES IN
THE ORDER GALLIFORMES. THESE ARE,
BROADLY SPEAKING, THE GAMEBIRDS OF
THE WORLD.**

To do this, in relation to these species and their effective
conservation, WPA

- Works to ensure their survival in their natural habitats.
- Fosters sound avicultural practice and captive breeding
  programmes, especially of species threatened in the
  wild.
- Establishes reserve collections and buffer stocks under
  WPA surveillance in collaboration with governments
  and approved breeders. Where suitably protected
  habitats can be ensured, re-introductions from such
  stocks can be undertaken.
- Has established a data bank and provides advice and
  information on all aspects of the species' ecology ,
  their breeding and conservation.
- Promotes and publishes research on the wild and
  captive populations.
- Educates the public about the birds and their
  environmental needs.
- Encourages above all the conservation of habitats, and
  supports and defends the integrity of sanctuaries,
  national parks and reserves of importance to the
  Galliformes in all countries.

W.P.A. PUBLICATIONS

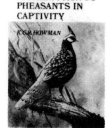

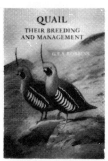

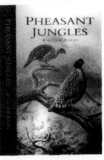

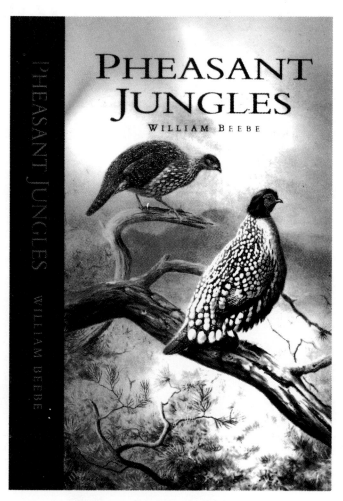

PHEASANT JUNGLES

Is a selection of Beebe's pheasant-tracking memoirs and experiences during a seventeen month pheasant hunting trip. Capturing the excitement of the solitary pursuit of these scarce and secretive birds, it also offers travel, at a time when wild places remained largely untouched by the ravages of development.

£19.95 + £2.50 p&p
for the UK and overseas surface rate